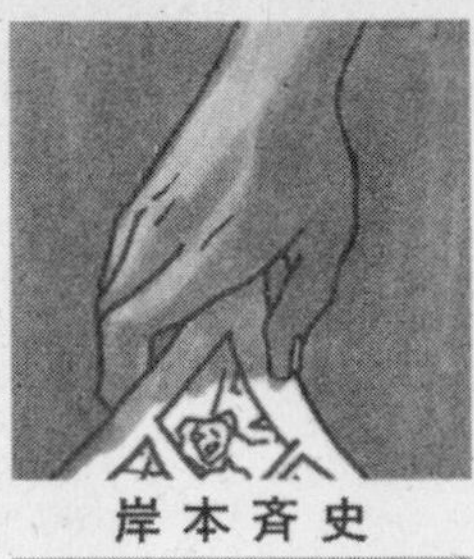

We're in the third volume of **Naruto**. I feel like I've developed a lot working on this title, but I still have a long way to go. My heart and body are still weak! I must devote a mountain of training to my work on **Naruto**! I want everyone to join me and share in the excitement of **Naruto**!

Masashi Kishimoto, 2000

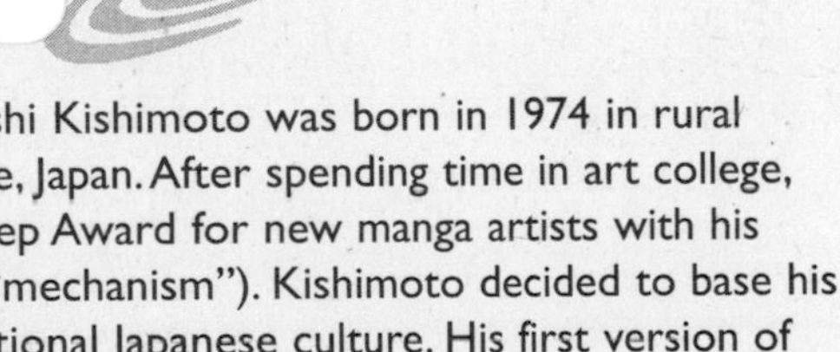

Author/artist Masashi Kishimoto was born in 1974 in rural Okayama Prefecture, Japan. After spending time in art college, he won the Hop Step Award for new manga artists with his manga **Karakuri** ("mechanism"). Kishimoto decided to base his next story on traditional Japanese culture. His first version of **Naruto**, drawn in 1997, was a one-shot story about fox spirits; his final version, which debuted in **Weekly Shonen Jump** in 1999, quickly became the most popular ninja manga in Japan.

NARUTO VOL. 3
The SHONEN JUMP Graphic Novel Edition

This graphic novel contains material that was originally published in English in **SHONEN JUMP** #11-14.

STORY AND ART BY
MASASHI KISHIMOTO

English Adaptation/Jo Duffy
Translation/Mari Morimoto
Touch-Up Art & Lettering/Heidi Szykowny
Cover & Graphics Design/Sean Lee
Senior Editor/Jason Thompson

Managing Editor/Elizabeth Kawasaki
Director of Production/Noboru Watanabe
Vice President of Publishing/Alvin Lu
Vice President & Editor in Chief/Yumi Hoashi
Sr. Director of Acquistions/Rika Inouye
Vice President of Sales & Marketing/Liza Coppola
Publisher/Hyoe Narita

Printed in the U.S.A.

Published by VIZ Media, LLC
P.O. Box 77010 • San Francisco, CA 94107

SHONEN JUMP Graphic Novel Edition
10 9 8 7 6
First printing, March 2004
Sixth printing, February 2006

PARENTAL ADVISORY
NARUTO is rated T for Teen and is recommended for ages 13 and up. This volume contains realistic & fantasy violence.

SHONEN JUMP GRAPHIC NOVEL

VOL. 3

BRIDGE OF COURAGE

STORY AND ART BY

MASASHI KISHIMOTO

SAKURA サクラ

Naruto and Sasuke's classmate. She has a crush on Sasuke, who ignores her. In return, she picks on Naruto, who has a crush on *her*.

NARUTO ナルト

When Naruto was an infant, he was used as a living sacrifice in a magic rite: a demonic fox spirit was sealed inside his body to keep it from wreaking havoc in the outside world. The orphan Naruto grew up to be an attention-seeking troublemaker. Despite the evil spirit inside him, he just wants to be the best ninja ever, and become the *Hokage*, the village champion.

SASUKE サスケ

The top student in Naruto's class, and a member of the prestigious Uchiha clan. His goal is to get revenge against a mysterious person who wronged him in the past.

KAKASHI カカシ

An upper-level ninja. His *sharingan* eye can deflect and duplicate enemy *ninjutsu*. Currently injured from his fight with Zabuza.

ZABUZA 再不斬

A sword-wielding assassin-ninja known as "the demon." Currently injured from his fight with Kakashi.

HAKU 白

Zabuza's consort, an agile young ninja of indeterminate gender.

TAZUNA タズナ

A grumpy old bridge-builder. He has a daughter, Tsunami, and a grandson, Inari.

THE STORY SO FAR...

Naruto, Sasuke and Sakura are a team of apprentice ninjas from the ninja village of Konohagakure. On their first big mission, they (and their trainer Kakashi) found themselves bodyguarding the bridgebuilder Tazuna on his way back home to the Land of the Waves. But Tazuna hadn't revealed that he was the target of professional hitmen, hired by the evil millionaire Gatô to keep him from finishing his bridge! In a desperate fight, the four ninja were able to defeat the assassin Zabuza—but a mysterious masked ninja stole Zabuza's body before the heroes realized he wasn't dead. Now, assassins and bodyguards are both preparing for a rematch...

NARUTO

VOL. 3
BRIDGE OF COURAGE

CONTENTS

Number 18: Training Day
CLIMB TREES --?!!
THAT'S RIGHT...
WHAT A WASTE OF TIME--!
HOW WOULD THAT QUALIFY AS TRAINING?
LISTEN UP, YOU THREE.

READ THIS WAY

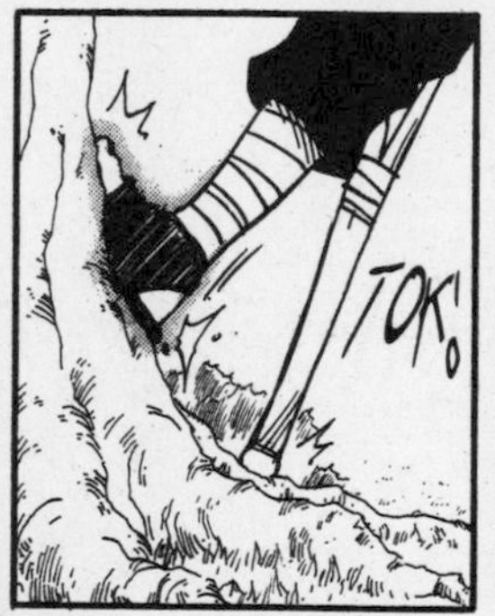

...
HE'S CLIMBING...
..WITH HIS LEGS... AND FEET... PARALLEL TO THE GROUND!

PHEW
THAT'S IT, IN A NUTSHELL.

FOCUS ALL OF THE ENERGY OF YOUR CHAKRA TOWARD THE SOLES OF YOUR FEET AND USE THAT POWER TO CLING TO THE TRUNK.
WHEN YOU HAVE FULL MASTERY OVER YOUR OWN CHAKRAS, THIS IS THE KIND OF THING YOU CAN ACCOMPLISH.

BUT... MASTER KAKASHI... HOW WILL LEARNING TO CLIMB TREES THIS WAY MAKE US ANY STRONGER?

I'M JUST GETTING TO THAT.
LISTEN AND LEARN.

THE POINT OF IT ALL, THE GOAL...

THAT SUBTLE CONTROL, IS THE MOST CRITICAL ASPECT OF EVERY *JUTSU* AND TECHNIQUE YOU'LL EVER APPLY.
...TO USE NO MORE THAN IS NECESSARY... BUT TO MAXIMIZE ITS EFFECTIVE-NESS IN WHERE AND HOW IT IS APPLIED.

...IS GREATER MASTERY OVER THE CHAKRAS.

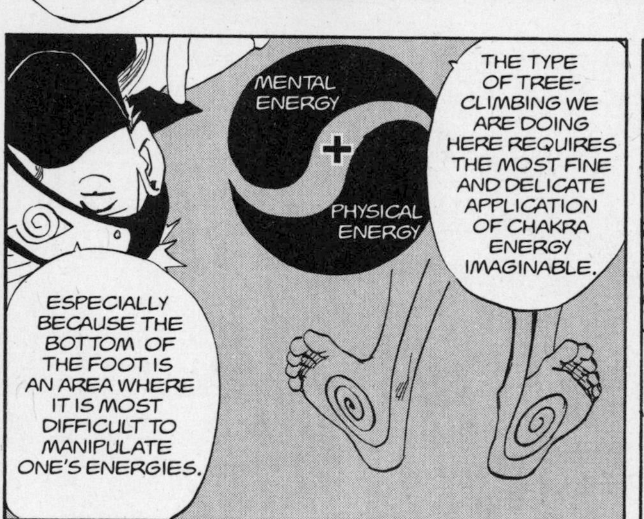
MENTAL ENERGY
+
PHYSICAL ENERGY
THE TYPE OF TREE-CLIMBING WE ARE DOING HERE REQUIRES THE MOST FINE AND DELICATE APPLICATION OF CHAKRA ENERGY IMAGINABLE.
ESPECIALLY BECAUSE THE BOTTOM OF THE FOOT IS AN AREA WHERE IT IS MOST DIFFICULT TO MANIPULATE ONE'S ENERGIES.

IT'S ALSO THE MOST DIFFICULT SKILL FOR EVEN A MASTER NINJA TO COMMAND.

OOH!

IN OTHER WORDS --
-- IF YOU CAN MASTER THE CONTROL NEEDED FOR THIS SKILL, NO *JUTSU* SHOULD EVER BE BEYOND YOU.
IN THEORY, ANYWAY.

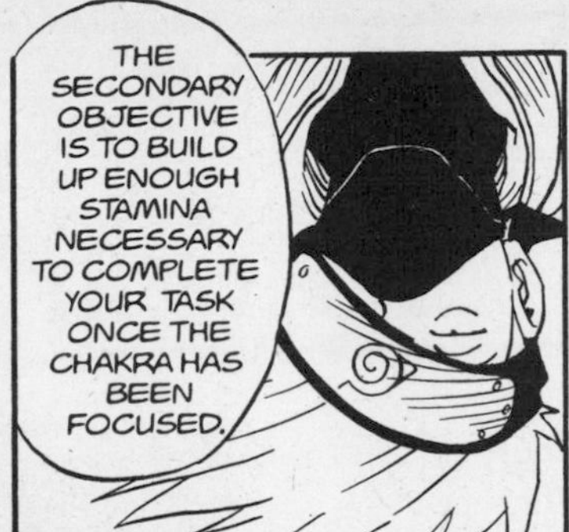
THE SECONDARY OBJECTIVE IS TO BUILD UP ENOUGH STAMINA NECESSARY TO COMPLETE YOUR TASK ONCE THE CHAKRA HAS BEEN FOCUSED.

IF YOU THINK **THIS** LOOKS HARD, IT'S EVEN MORE DIFFICULT...
...TO MAINTAIN YOUR CHAKRA WHEN USING NINJUTSU.

IN BATTLE, CIRCUMSTANCES ARE CONSTANTLY CHANGING, AND A TRUE SHINOBI HAS TO BE ABLE TO MANIPULATE AND MAINTAIN HIS CHAKRAS ON THE FLY, IF HE EVER HOPES TO PREVAIL.
THE TIME YOU NEED TO JUST STAND AROUND TRYING TO SUMMON AND CONTROL YOUR OWN POWERS IS A LUXURY YOU WON'T HAVE.

SO WHILE YOU'RE CLIMBING THOSE TREES...
...YOU'LL ALSO BE MASTERING SKILLS THAT WILL PROBABLY SAVE YOUR LIVES.

FWUP
...NOW, NO MORE TALK. IT'S TIME FOR ACTION.

FLIP

THE ONLY WAY TO LEARN IS BY DOING.

USE THE *KUNAI* BLADES TO SCORE THE BARK AT THE HIGHEST POINT YOU CAN CLIMB TO. IT WILL SERVE AS A REMINDER FOR LATER.

!
!
!
THOK
THOK
THOK

YOUR GOAL IS TO MAKE A MARK ON A HIGHER SPOT EACH TIME YOU CLIMB.
I DON'T EXPECT ANY OF YOU TO REACH THE TREETOP ON YOUR FIRST TRY.
A RUNNING START WILL PROBABLY GIVE ENOUGH MOMENTUM FOR A GOOD FIRST EFFORT. ALL RIGHT?

READ THIS WAY
NO SWEAT!!
SMAT
I COULD DO THIS ONE BEFORE BREAKFAST!
I'M THE FASTEST-DEVELOPING NINJA ON THIS TEAM!
...
LESS TALK AND MORE ACTION.
CHOOSE YOUR TREES AND UP YOU GO!
RIGHT-
FOCUS MY CHAKRA IN MY FEET...
OOOOOHMM
READY OR NOT, HERE I COME!!
MMMMMMM
TAK TAK TAK TAK
THOMP

OWWW..!!!
WHOOP
TOK
TOK
TOK
TOK

RRR...

CRUNCH
ACK..!
SHIP

CHUK!!

GRRR

FWUP

TAP

MAINTAINING FOCUS IS A LOT HARDER THAN I EXPECTED...

TOO LITTLE, AND YOU'LL NEVER ADHERE IN THE FIRST PLACE...
...SO YOU END UP LIKE NARUTO.
AAARGH!!!
FLP FLP

TOO MUCH FORCE AND THE SURFACE'S OWN ENERGY REPELS YOU.

THIS IS EASIER THAN I THOUGHT!
!

THERE IS THE DIFFERENCE BETWEEN NARUTO AND SASUKE IN A NUTSHELL.
HUH...!

SAKURA...?!

GIGGLE

WELL, NOW WE KNOW WHICH OF YOU THREE HAS THE BEST CONTROL OVER HER CHAKRAS.

OUR YOUNG LADY.

SIGH
I WANTED TO IMPRESS SASUKE... BUT THE ONLY ONE WHO CARED WAS NARUTO...
...JUST LIKE ALWAYS!

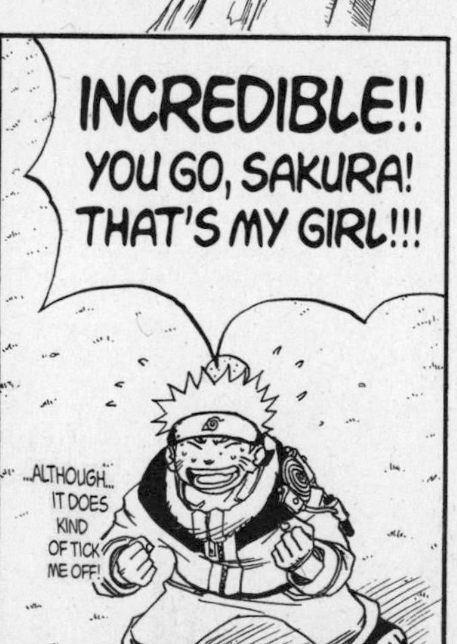

INCREDIBLE!! YOU GO, SAKURA! THAT'S MY GIRL!!!
...ALTHOUGH... IT DOES KIND OF TICK ME OFF!

WELL...! UNDERSTANDING THE USE OF ONE'S CHAKRAS AND MANIPULATING THEM, SUCCESSFULLY...
...IS QUITE AN ACHIEVEMENT. SO FAR...

... SAKURA IS PROBABLY THE ONE CLOSEST TO OVERTAKING OUR LEADER, LORD HOKAGE...
DESPITE ALL OF NARUTO'S BOASTS AND ASPIRATIONS...

AND THE FINEST HOPE OF CLAN UCHIHA DOESN'T SEEM TOO IMPRESSIVE, EITHER.
STAB

MASTER KAKASHI, HOW COULD YOU?!
SASUKE'S GOING TO HATE ME!

ON THE OTHER HAND...
WITHIN THEM, NARUTO AND SASUKE BOTH HARBOR SUCH MASSIVE, UNTAPPED RESERVES OF CHAKRA THAT SAKURA'S IS NOTHING BY COMPARISON.

IF THIS LESSON GOES AS PLANNED...
... BY THE END, WE SHOULD BE ABLE TO TAP THOSE VAST RESOURCES.

ALL RIGHT--!
FOR STARTERS, AT LEAST I CAN CATCH UP WITH SASUKE!
GRR
RRR
AND I WILL!!

...

SKUF

HAH!!
THEY'RE WASTING THEIR TIME...

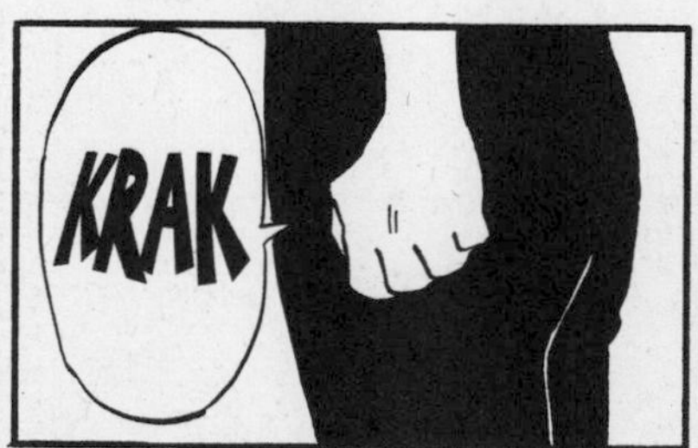
KRAK

KREEEAK
NINJA FROM THE LAND OF THE MIST WOULD APPEAR TO BE VASTLY OVERRATED.
I'M SURPRISED YOU HAVE THE NERVE TO SHOW YOUR FACE AROUND HERE AFTER TAKING A BEATING LIKE THAT.
ZOURI SAMURAI BODYGUARD IN THE SERVICE OF GATÔ
WARAJI SAMURAI BODYGUARD IN THE SERVICE OF GATÔ

YOU CAN'T EVEN CLEAN UP FOR YOUR MISERABLE SUBORDINATES. "DEMON"... YEAH RIGHT!
DON'T MAKE ME LAUGH.
...
RRRR
POK
RR
...
ARE THEY GOING TO ATTACK...?
WAIT A MINUTE, YOU TWO...
SHFF
SO...
TAK
TAK
NOTHING TO SAY FOR YOURSELF?

NO LAST WORDS?
!
GRAB
AAARGH!!!
DON'T DEFILE LORD ZABUZA WITH YOUR TOUCH.
HOW DARE YOU?!

!!

!!

N-NO...
HE DIDN'T EVEN SEEM TO MOVE...!

YOU DON'T WANT TO DO THAT...
... WHEN I'M ANGRY.

HE'S SOME KIND OF MONSTER...
TH-THERE HAD BETTER NOT BE ANY MORE MISTAKES.
I-IF YOU FAIL AGAIN, DON'T THINK YOU CAN COME BACK HERE!
MY... SWORD...
I'M GOING
SHF
KLANG
SLAM
SIGH
HAKU... THERE WAS NO NEED FOR YOU TO...
I KNOW...
BUT IT'S TOO SOON TO FINISH GATÔ OFF.
IF WE CAUSE A COMMOTION WHERE WE ARE, WE MIGHT FIND OURSELVES ON THE RUN FROM THEM AGAIN.
FOR NOW, LET'S BE PATIENT.
AHHH..
...YES!

READ THIS WAY

AAAAAH..!
OWW..!!

TWITCH
TWITCH
OOH
OOH
HUFF
HUFF
PUFF

HUFF
PUFF
HUFF

HUFF
HUFF
HUFF
HUFF

...I'M... EXHAUSTED!
THE BOYS HAVE SO MUCH STAMINA...
HUFF
BUT NARUTO HASN'T IMPROVED ONE BIT!
NOW HE'LL PROBABLY HAVE A TANTRUM AND QUIT!
DAMN!

DANG IT!
CRUNCH
I KNEW IT!
HE'S SO PREDICTABLE...

HEY, HEY! SAKURA! COULD YOU HELP ME GET THE HANG OF THIS?
HUNH?

NARUTO'S DEVELOPING... GROWING UP.
I WONDER HOW STRONG HE'LL BECOME.

IF HE ONLY KNEW!
HIS LATENT ABILITIES DWARF EVEN THOSE OF SASUKE...
...AND, PERHAPS MINE, AS WELL!
THAT WOULD BE A MARVEL... AND A PLEASURE!

A boy who is as isolated and lonely as Naruto.

EARLY CHARACTER DESIGNS

This was the original design for the character of Sasuke. It's hardly changed at all over time.

The main difference is the absence of the talisman he wore around his neck. In general, whenever I come up with a new character, my initial impulse is so use as much line and ornamentation as possible until the visual concept is in danger of becoming lost amid the busy, little details.

This is especially true of principal characters. I get so caught up in what I'm doing with them, I make things much too difficult for myself; until I finally have the sense to step back and ask myself, "Am I really going to be able to draw such a fussy, complicated character over and over, panel after panel, and issue after issue, week in and week out?"

There was far too much going on visually with Sasuke, and too many lines overall, so I simplified him into a good, basic contrast to Naruto's visual image.

Sasuke is a particular challenge for me to draw even now, because he is a young and rather pretty boy, but if I'm not careful he loses his youthful quality and I end up drawing him like a much older boy or a grown man. I've never had a character like him in one of my comics before—that kind of boy on the cusp of manhood, who's somehow mature and handsome beyond his years.

Keeping the visual consistently right makes him the character who takes the most work and energy from me. Maybe that's why he's become my favorite character.

Number 19: The Emblem of Courage

YAWWWN
BORRRRING!
KLONK
KLONK
KLANK
BAM
BAM
RATCH
RATCH

SIGH
SKF

ALL ALONE AND LONESOME?

WHERE ARE BLONDIE AND PRETTY-BOY?

TRAINING.
THEN WHY AREN'T YOU WITH THEM?

I SURPASSED THEM.
MASTER KAKASHI TOLD ME TO STAY HERE AND PROTECT YOU.

REALLY...?
...

READ THIS WAY

GRUNT
TAZUNA...
CAN I TALK TO YOU?

HUNH?
WHAT'S WRONG, GIICHI?

I'VE BEEN THINKING IT OVER... THIS BRIDGE WE'RE WORKING ON...
I WANT OFF THE JOB!

WH-WHY?!
OUT OF NOWHERE LIKE THIS... YOU, OF ALL PEOPLE!!

TAZUNA! WE GO BACK A LONG WAY.

I WANT TO HELP YOU, BUT WE CAN'T TAKE THIS RISK. GATÔ WILL TAKE OUT A CONTRACT ON US IF WE DON'T STOP!
AND IF YOU DIE, IT WON'T JUST BE THIS ONE PROJECT. WE COULD ALL LOSE EVERYTHING!

PLEASE, JUST GIVE IT UP...
THE BRIDGE ISN'T WORTH IT.

...

I CAN'T DO THAT.

THIS BRIDGE BELONGS TO US ALL.
IT'S EVERYTHING WE'VE BEEN WORKING TOWARD, FOR OUR ENTIRE CITY.
WHEN IT'S FINISHED, IT WILL BRING TRADE AND COMMERCE AND AFFLUENCE TO US, AND PUT OUR POOR, LITTLE LAND OF THE WAVES ON THE MAP!

BUT WE'RE TALKING ABOUT **LIVES** HERE. **YOUR** LIFE!
IT'S AFTERNOON NOW ALREADY, ISN'T IT? LET'S CALL IT A DAY.

第三
GIICHI... YOU DON'T HAVE TO COME BACK.

MY DAUGHTER ASKED ME TO PICK UP SOME THINGS FOR OUR LUNCH ON THE WAY HOME, SO...
STOP, THIEF!!

RUSH
RUSSH
WILL DO ANY JOB YOU WANT

WHAT'S WRONG WITH THIS TOWN?

HE'S JUST A KID...
HERE WE ARE!

GROCERY
八百屋
DONT PISS HERE
WELCOME!

THIS STORE HAS ALMOST NOTHING IN IT!

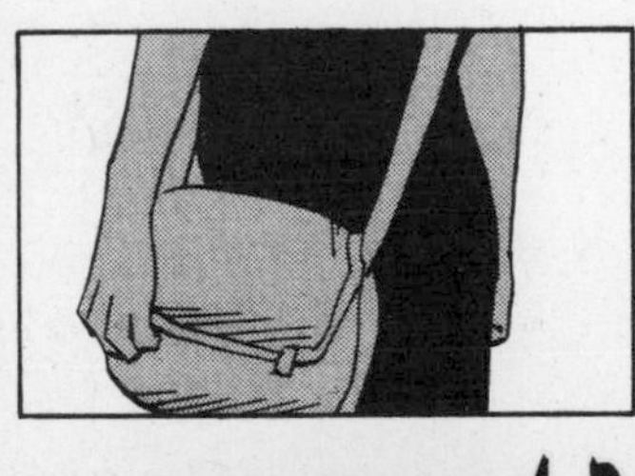

GRAB

HUH?!
!!

PERVERT-!!

N-NO...

HYAAH--!!

WOW

IT'S BEEN LIKE THIS EVER SINCE GATÔ MOVED IN.
TAK

WE'VE BECOME A CITY OF SLACKERS, COWARDS, AND FOOLS!
...

THAT'S WHY THE BRIDGE WE ARE BUILDING IS SO ESSENTIAL!
IT WILL BE AN EMBLEM OF COURAGE. MAYBE THE PEOPLE WHO'VE TAKEN THE PATH OF LEAST RESISTANCE WILL BE WILLING TO WALK THE ROAD OF COURAGE AND DIGNITY AGAIN.

IF WE CAN ONLY COMPLETE IT...
I TRULY BELIEVE THAT OUR CITY AND OUR PEOPLE CAN BE WHAT THEY ONCE WERE AGAIN!

SASUKE... NARUTO...

YAAAAH!!
TAK
TAK
TAK
TAK
TAK
TAK
TAK
TAK

TAP
SLIP
SLICE
!
TAK
TAK
TAK
TAK
TAK
TAK
TAK

THAT JERK SASUKE IS STILL CLIMBING!
HUFF
HUFF
HUFF
GRRR! HE'S STILL HIGHER THAN ME!

SLASH
SLIP
!
TOK
TOK
TOK
OH...!
CRAP...! HE'S CATCHING UP...

DARN IT--!
THUK

HEY... WAIT A MINUTE!
I CAN'T LET SASUKE DISTRACT ME.
RATTLE
RATTLE
I NEED TOTAL CONCEN-TRATION.

HEY! SAKURA! COULD YOU HELP ME GET THE HANG OF THIS?
YOU'RE HOPELESS!

NOW, PAY ATTENTION. IT TAKES MENTAL ENERGY TO GENERATE AND MANIPULATE CHAKRA, SO IF YOU GET ALL STRESSED OUT OR DISTRACTED, YOU CAN'T DO IT.
TAKE IT EASY. RELAX AND FOCUS ON THE TREE UNTIL YOU CAN FEEL HOW MUCH OR HOW LITTLE ENERGY YOU'LL NEED TO CENTER IN THE SOLES OF YOUR FEET.

RIGHT! FOCUS. CONCENTRATE. I CAN DO THAT. I KNOW I CAN!

THIS TIME FOR SURE!

HEY, NARUTO!
THUD!

YOU... YOU... YOU--!!

WANNA FIGHT?
YOU'RE BREAKING MY CONCENTRATION! STOP BUGGING ME!

WHAT?!

...
UHHH... WELL....

WH-... WHAT? WHAT IS IT?
WHY'S HE WANT TO TALK TO ME ALL OF A SUDDEN?

WH...
WHAT DID SAKURA SAY TO YOU...?

!?

YEAH!!!

NONE OF YOUR BUSINESS!
OW!

...
SHH-----I

I CAN'T REMEMBER THE LAST TIME I SHARED A MEAL WITH SO MANY PEOPLE!!
BOY, THIS IS REAL FUN!
KLAT
KLAT

MUNCH
MUNCH

MNUCH
GULP

MORE, PLEASE!
SHF
SHF
SCOWL
SCOWL
!

ULP..!
?

BLORTCH
...

STOP EATING IF YOU'RE JUST GONNA HURL IT BACK UP!
SMAK
HUFF
HUFF
HUFF
HUFF

... NO, I WANNA EAT!

HEH...
BECAUSE EVEN IF WE MAKE OURSELVES SICK TO DO IT, WE HAVE TO EAT IF WE WANT TO GET STRONG!

WHATEVER IT TAKES!
THROWING UP, HOWEVER, IS AN ENTIRELY DIFFERENT SITUATION...♡

UM— WHY IS THIS PICTURE TORN?

LITTLE INARI WAS LOOKING AT THIS THE WHOLE TIME WE WERE HAVING DINNER.
SOMEONE'S FACE IS COMPLETELY GONE. IS THAT DELIBERATE?
!

!

READ THIS WAY

...

...IT WAS A PICTURE OF INARI'S FATHER.

...ONCE UPON A TIME, IF YOU WILL...
...OUR ENTIRE CITY CALLED HIM A HERO.

SHOVE

SHHF

INARI! ...
WHERE ARE YOU GOING?

SLAM!

INARI!

READ THIS WAY

FATHER! I'VE TOLD YOU TIME AND AGAIN NOT TO MENTION THAT IN FRONT OF MY SON!!

...
SO... YOU'RE TALKING ABOUT WHAT IT IS THAT MAKES INARI ACT SO STRANGELY...?

IT SOUNDS LIKE THERE'S A STORY THERE...
...

...THE MAN IN THE PICTURE WAS NOT INARI'S BIRTH FATHER...
BUT THEY WERE AS LOVING AND CLOSE AS ANY BIOLOGICAL FATHER AND SON COULD HAVE BEEN.
INARI WAS SUCH A HAPPY, LAUGHING CHILD BACK THEN...

READ THIS WAY

SOB SOB
?

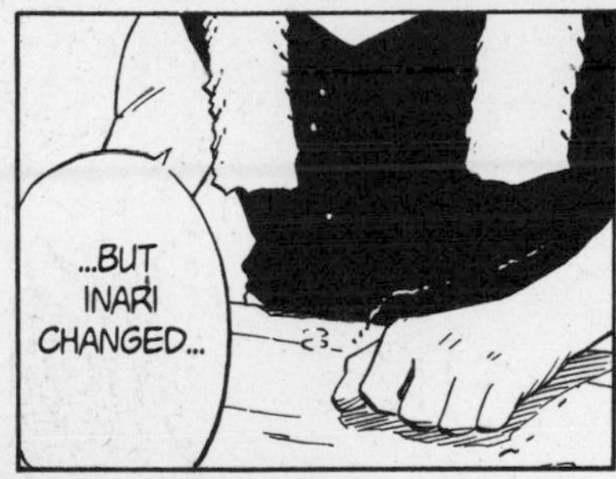
...BUT INARI CHANGED...

...AFTER WHAT HAPPENED TO HIS FATHER.

Number 20: The Land That Had a Hero...!!

OUR PEOPLE - AND ESPECIALLY LITTLE INARI - WERE ROBBED OF THE VERY MEANING OF COURAGE...
...BECAUSE OF WHAT HAPPENED THAT DAY.

"WHAT HAPPENED"?
WHAT WAS IT? WHAT COULD HAVE CHANGED INARI SO MUCH?

!
!
!
!

...

LET ME START AT THE BEGINNING... AND TELL YOU ABOUT THE MAN WHO OUR ENTIRE LAND CALLED A CHAMPION AND A HERO.
WIPE

"CHAMPION"...?

IT WAS ABOUT THREE YEARS AGO...
HERE, POOCHIE!!
...THAT INARI AND THE MAN FIRST MET.
NOT ANY MORE! STARTING NOW, HIS NAME IS SHOOTING STAR... AND HE BELONGS TO ME!!
HE'S NOT A SHOOTING STAR!! THAT'S MY POOCHIE!!
GIVE HIM BACK!!
POOCHIE'S MY FRIEND!
YOU CAN'T HAVE HIM!!
SHUT UP--!!
...
SLASH
NYAH!!
PLOP
WOOF!?
HAH!

SPLOOSH
!!
SPLASH
SPLASH
POOCHIE--!!
YIPE! YIPE!
IT'S WHAT YOU GET FOR NOT HANDING HIM OVER WHEN I ORDERED.
WHO CARES ABOUT A DUMB DOG, ANYWAY?
HEY!! LET INARI GO!
YOU CAN'T JUST DROWN MY DOG!
SPLASH
WELL, IF THE PUPPY MEANS SO MUCH TO YOU...
... BETTER GO SAVE HIM!!
BUT...
WELL, WHAT ARE YOU WAITING FOR?
ARE YOU GOING TO LET HIM JUST DIE?!!

POOCHIE'S MY BEST FRIEND!!
OF COURSE NOT!!!
SPLASH SPLASH
BUT... BUT...
I'M SORRY, POOCHIE...
SHUDDER SHUDDER
I DON'T KNOW HOW TO SWIM...
HEY!! IF YOU OWN HIM, WHY AREN'T YOU DIVING IN?
TAK
BOOT
AAGGH!
THIS AIN'T RIGHT, AKANE. WHAT IF HE CAN'T SWIM?
SPLOOSH
GAKK--!
H-HELP! HELP ME!

AW, JUST LEAVE HIM!
B-... BUT...
OR DO YOU WANT TO BE THE NEXT ONE PERFORMING A LITTLE PET RESCUE?
GLUB!!
I-I DON'T WANNA DIE...
S-SOMEBODY, HELP...!!
SPLASH
!
P...POOCHIE--?!
WOOF!!
FLAP
FLOP
PADDLE
PADDLE
BUT, I DIGRESS...
P-P-P--!!!
hum de dum
SPLASH
NECESSITY, AND THE NEARNESS OF HIS OWN DEATH FINALLY TAUGHT POOCHIE HOW TO DOG PADDLE...
P-POOCHIE--!!

SHAKE
WHAT--!!
SHAKE
SHAKE
SHAKE
SHOOTING STAR'S GETTING AWAY. GO AFTER HIM!!!
WOOF!
POOCHIE--!!
GLUR
OHH...
GLUB
I-...IT HURTS
THIS IS IT...
I'M...
DYING...
GLEAM
ARE YOU AWAKE, SON?
!!
MMMF

KRACKLE
KRACKLE
I REALLY LET THOSE PUNKS WHO WERE PICKING ON YOU HAVE IT GOOD.
HERE, EAT!
...GOD?
NO... MAYBE NOT...
DID YOU... RESCUE ME, MISTER?!
...
...YOU'VE HAD A PRETTY ROUGH TIME OF IT, HAVEN'T YOU?!
...EVEN YOUR DOG LET YOU DOWN. WHERE I COME FROM, DOGS ARE LOYAL. YOU CAN COUNT ON THEM. BUT...
MUNCH
MUNCH
WELL, I GUESS, SINCE YOU LET HIM DOWN FIRST, WE REALLY SHOULDN'T BE TOO HARD ON HIM.
SLURP
...!...

I WAS TOO SCARED TO EVEN MOVE.
SNIFF
!
...
I WANTED TO RESCUE HIM...
BUT... I GUESS I WASN'T BRAVE ENOUGH.
PAT
...OF COURSE NOT... ANY KID YOUR AGE WOULD HAVE BEEN TERRIFIED.
PAT
BUT KEEP IN MIND, SON...
HUH...?
...WHEN YOU DO BECOME A MAN, YOU HAVE TO WALK A ROAD THAT WON'T LEAVE YOU FILLED WITH REGRETS.
?

IF SOMETHING IS PRECIOUS TO YOU...

NO MATTER HOW PAINFUL OR HOW HARD IT SEEMS, NO MATTER WHAT IT MAY COST YOU, YOU HAVE TO HANG IN THERE...

FLEX

...AND PROTECT IT WITH ALL THE STRENGTH YOU'VE GOT, EVEN AT THE RISK OF YOUR OWN LIFE!

IF YOU DO THAT, THEN EVEN IF YOU DIE IN THE ATTEMPT, AT LEAST THE WORLD WILL BE LEFT WITH THE PROOF THAT A MAN WORTH LIVING HAD DIED!

IT'D BE LIKE YOUR LEGACY...

RIGHT?!

OKAY... I GUESS IT DOES SOUND A LITTLE CORNY, HUNH?

YEAH!!

HIS NAME WAS KAIZA. HE WAS A FISHERMAN WHO CAME HERE FROM ABROAD TO SEEK HIS FORTUNE.

HEY! I FINALLY GOT A SMILE OUT OF YOU! NOW EAT. EAT!

OH!

FROM THAT DAY FORWARD, INARI'S AFFECTION AND ADMIRATION FOR KAIZA GREW AND GREW.

YANK

YANK

IT PROBABLY HAD SOMETHING TO DO WITH INARI'S REAL FATHEF HAVING DIED BEFORE THE BOY WAS OLD ENOUGH TO REMEMBE HIM, BUT EVEN SO... THAT BOY STU TO KAIZA LIKE WHITE ON RICE.
THEY WERE ALWAYS TOGETHER, LIKE ANY OTHER FATHER AND SON.
HOW IS IT GOING, YOU TWO?
IN NO TIME AT ALL, KAIZA WAS LIKE ONE OF THE FAMILY.

PITTER PITTER

AND HE WAS JUST THE KIND OF MAN THIS TOWN NEEDS MORE OF!

I-...**IT'S TERRIBLE!!** KAIZA, THE RAIN'S SO HEAVY, IT'S OVERFLOWED THE RIVERBANKS AND FORCED OPEN ALL OF THE LOCKS!!

SLAM

AT THIS RATE, ALL OF SECTOR D WILL BE FLOODED!!
WHAT?!!
DADDY!!
INARI, GO TO THE BACK AND GET THE ROPES!
OKAY!
RRRUMBLE
THIS IS AWFUL—THE ONLY WAY WE COULD POSSIBLY GET THIS LOCK CLOSED IS IF WE PUT A ROPE AROUND THE ENTIRE BARRIER AND PULL IT, BUT...
IMPOSSIBLE! HOW WOULD WE GET A ROPE AROUND IT IN THE FIRST PLACE!! ANYONE WHO GOES INTO THAT TORRENT WILL BE SWEPT AWAY AND DROWNED!!
THE LONGER WE WAIT, THE WORSE IT WILL GET... AND SECTOR D IS RUNNING OUT OF TIME!
I'LL GO!

KAIZA!!
IT CAN'T BE DONE, MAN!!
YOU'LL BE THROWING YOUR LIFE AWAY!!
DON'T RISK IT!
DADDY!!
DON'T WORRY, INARI... DADDY CAN DO ANYTHING!
TAK
PAT!
BECAUSE HE LOVES THE CITY WHERE HIS LITTLE BOY LIVES!
SKFF

LEAP
KAIZA!!
IF SOMETHING IS PRECIOUS TO YOU.....
SPLASH
PROTECT IT WITH ALL THE STRENGTH YOU'VE GOT...
EVEN AT THE RISK...
...OF YOUR OWN LIFE!
GO, DADDY--!!
HE'S DONE IT!!! THE ROPE'S IN PLACE!!
PULL EVERYONE. PULL!
THAT WAS WHEN...

READ THIS WAY

...PEOPLE HERE STARTED CALLING KAIZA A CHAMPION AND A HERO.
WITH A FATHER LIKE THAT, INARI COULD HOLD HIS HEAD UP HIGH.
...UNTIL GATÔ CAME TO TOWN...

...AND THE INCIDENT YOU'VE ALLUDED TO TOOK PLACE...

SO... WHAT HAPPENED?

IN FRONT OF THE ENTIRE CITY...
GATÔ HAD KAIZA PUT TO DEATH!

WHAT?
EVERYBODY LISTEN UP! THIS MAN HAS COMMITED ACTS OF VIOLENCE AND TERRORISM AGAINST MY COMPANY AND OUR ACTIVITIES HERE.
...
UHHN
HE'S OPENLY DENOUNCED OUR POLICIES AND TRIED TO INCITE SABOTAGE AND RESISTANCE AGAINST US, AND DISRUPTED THE ORDER OF THIS LAND. THE PENALTY FOR ALL HIS CRIMES IS DEATH. THE SENTENCE WILL BE CARRIED OUT AT ONCE...
GASP
GASP
GASP
...TO ENSURE THAT SUCH AN AWFUL THING WILL NEVER DISTURB ANY OF US, EVER AGAIN!
DADDY!!
INARI!

NOW!
HMMF
POK
SHING
DADDY..!!
BUT... YOU PROMISED... YOU PROMISED TO PROTECT ME!
...YOU'RE A LIAR!!
EVER SINCE THEN, INARI HAS CHANGED...
AND TSUNAMI... AND EVERYONE IN THE CITY'S CHANGED, TOO.

"HERO"? YOU'RE DUMB!
THERE'S NO SUCH THING!!!

CLATTER

SOB
SOB
...DADDY...

...DON'T EVEN THINK ABOUT TRAINING ANY MORE TODAY. IF YOU TRY TO WORK YOUR CHAKRAS ANY MORE WITH GETTING SOME REST FIRST, IT WOULD PROBABLY KILL YOU.

WHAT ARE YOU DOING, NARUTO...?
!
SPLAT
OW!

!

I'M GOING TO PROVE TO HIM THAT HE'S WRONG!
?
PROVE WHAT? TO WHOM?
BAM
I'M GOING TO SHOW INARI...!
THAT THERE ARE STILL HEROES IN THE WORLD!!!

Number 21: A Meeting in the Forest...!!
MORNING ON THE SIXTH DAY OF TRAINING...
TWEET
TWEET
TWEET
ZZZZZZZZZZ
ZZZZZZZZZ
TWEET
SSHF
FLUFF

TWEET
TWEET

TWEET
SNAP

FLAP

!

FLAP
OH!

FLAP
PECK
PECK

...

FLOP
grumble

!

WHAT'S GOING ON HERE?!!
WHO ARE YOU?!!

TAK

SHF

FLAP
FLAP
FLAP
FLAP

-YA-AAAWN-
MMMM
NAUGHTY NARUTO STAYED OUT ALL NIGHT AGAIN, DIDN'T HE?
EVER SINCE YOU TOLD US THAT STORY, HE'S BEEN IN THE TREES, TRAINING ALL ALONE, NIGHT AFTER NIGHT...
...AN IDIOT WITH AN OBSESSION!
IF HE EXHAUSTS HIS CHAKRA, HE COULD KILL HIMSELF... AND BE LYING DEAD SOMEWHERE RIGHT NOW.
...I HOPE HE'S ALL RIGHT. IT'S NOT GOOD FOR A BOY TO SPEND NIGHT AFTER NIGHT ALONE OUTSIDE!
THERE'S NOTHING TO WORRY ABOUT.
NARUTO'S A GOOFY KID... BUT HE'S ALSO A FULL-FLEDGED NINJA.

READ THIS WAY

IS IT POSSIBLE... COULD HE HAVE KILLED HIMSELF?
THAT BONE-HEAD...

YOU'LL CATCH YOUR DEATH OF COLD, SLEEPING ON THE GROUND.
TAP
...HUNH?

THAT'S SOME JOB YOU TOOK ON, GIRL... HARVESTING ALL THAT THIS EARLY IN THE MORNING.
LOOK AT WHO'S TALKING! WHAT WERE YOU DOING IN THE MIDDLE OF NOWHERE AT THE CRACK OF DAWN?

I'M SORRY TO HAVE IMPOSED ON YOU.
ARE THESE GRASSES AND WEEDS REALLY MEDICINAL?

!

TRAINING!!

YEAH
WHY? DO YOU THINK I LOOK LIKE ONE? DO I? REALLY? BECAUSE I AM!

REALLY? THAT HEADBAND YOU'RE WEARING... ARE YOU SOME KIND OF NINJA?
!!
PING!

WOW—THAT'S INCREDIBLE!

HEH HEH...

WHAT ARE YOU TRAINING FOR?

TO BUILD UP MY STRENGTH.

BUT... BUT YOU LOOK SO STRONG AND MANLY ALREADY!
NOPE! WRONG!! I NEED TO BE A LOT STRONGER THAN THIS!

TO BECOME TOP DOG IN MY HOME TOWN!

ALL THE PEOPLE WHO USED TO TREAT ME LIKE DIRT WILL HAVE TO SAY "HE'S THE NUMBER ONE NINJA"!

AND RIGHT AT THE MOMENT, I KIND OF HAVE TO PROVE A POINT... TO A CERTAIN PERSON I KNOW.

...ARE YOU DOING THIS FOR THE SAKE OF THAT PERSON...
...OR FOR YOUR OWN SATISFACTION?

...
...WHUT?

...
·TEE-HEE·

!
GLARE

WHAT'S SO FUNNY?

...DO YOU HAVE...
...ANYONE SPECIAL IN YOUR LIFE?

!
?
WHAT'S THIS GIRL DRIVING AT?...

!?

TAK

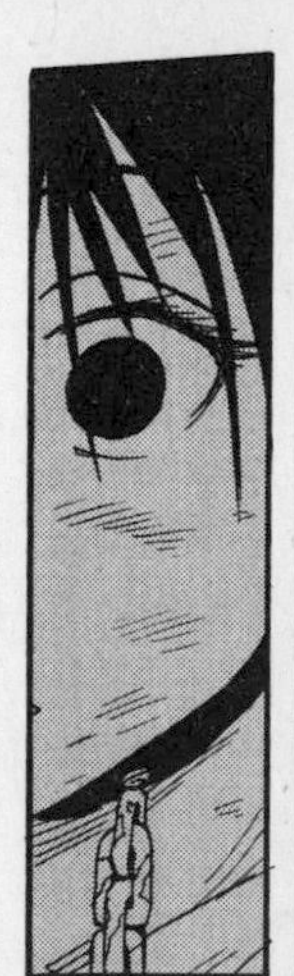

READ THIS WAY

...

?
WHAT NOW?

WHEN PEOPLE...
...ARE PROTECTING SOMETHING TRULY PRECIOUS TO THEM, THEY TRULY CAN BECOME...
...AS STRONG AS THEY MUST BE!

...

DADDY... LOVES THE CITY WHERE HIS LITTLE BOY LIVES!
I WILL NEVER LET MY COMRADES DIE!
KEEP AWAY FROM MASTER IRUKA...
...OR I'LL KILL YOU!

YUP!
I KNOW ALL ABOUT IT!
GR
IN

SHF

YOU **WILL** GET STRONGER...
I KNOW WE'LL MEET AGAIN...
RIGHT!

...SO...
...YOU SHOULD KNOW...

I'M A BOY.
!

WHOA-·!!
HE'S... HE'S EVEN GIRLIER THAN SAKURA!
NO WAY!

SHF

...

THE WORLD IS AN AMAZING PLACE SOMETIMES!
?

THE NEXT MORNING -- THE SEVENTH DAY OF TRAINING

WHERE DID NARUTO GO **THIS** TIME...?
PUSHING HIMSELF BEYOND HIS LIMIT, GOING OUT BY HIMSELF AGAIN LAST NIGHT...
AND AT BREAKFAST TIME...
...SASUKE SAYS HE'S GOING FOR A WALK... AND HE DISAPPEARS, TOO!

!
!
THOK

!
!

TA-DAAA
HUFF
PUFF
HEH-HEH...

DID YOU SEE?
LOOKIT HOW HIGH I CAN GO!!
WELL?! WELL?!

AMAZING!...
NARUTO CAN CLIMB ALL THE WAY UP THERE?

...HUNH!

READ THIS WAY

ALLEZ...

SLIP
OO-OOPS!
SLIDE
!

WHU-OH!

YOU IDIOT!!!
!!
NO!!!
IF HE FALLS FROM THAT HEIGHT...!!

YIPE!!!

AIEE--!!
I'M NOT HEALED ENOUGH TO --!

TA-DAAAH!

PSYCH--!!

HEH...

HAH... GOTCHA, SUCKERS!!
HA-HA!
...
...

YOU... YOU... ALMOST GAVE ME A HEART ATTACK, YOU JERK!
OH, YEAH!
INNER SAKURA
I'M GONNA KILL YOU FOR THIS... LATER!

POOFF
UH--!

UH-OH!!

AGH!!!
HEY--!!
TWICE IS TOO MUCH, NARUTO! STOP MESSING AROUND!!!

YAAAA-
-AAAAAAH-
SMAP
GRAB!!
YOU BONE-HEAD.
OW!

SPLISH
SPLASH

...UZUMAKI NARUTO, HUH...

196...
197...
198...

...I KEEP MEANING TO ASK YOU...
YOU KNOW I DUPED YOU ABOUT HOW DANGEROUS THIS MISSION WAS TO GET YOU TO COME HERE...
... SO WHY DO YOU STAY?
"TO KNOW WHAT IS RIGHT AND CHOOSE TO IGNORE IT IS THE ACT OF A COWARD."

"LIKE MASTER, LIKE MAN!"

THOSE ARE THE TEACHINGS OF SOME OF OUR PREVIOUS LORDS HOKAGE.
199
GRUNT

IT LOOKS LIKE I'M ALMOST COMPLETELY HEALED.
TRUE SHINOBI DO NOT MERELY DANCE TO THE TUNE OF WHOEVER PAYS THE PIPER.

THIS IS THE SHINOBI WAY OF LIFE...

MOST OF YOUR STRENGTH HAS RETURNED.
SLOP

KRUNCH

OF COURSE.

EXCELLENT!!

LET'S GET GOING, HAKU!

DRIP

DRIP

NARUTO

Number 22: The Enemies Return
PUFF
PUFF
WANT TO HEAD BACK?
SURE!!
HUFF

KREAK
SO, YOU'RE FINALLY BACK!
LOOKING LIKE SOMETHING THE CAT DRAGGED IN!
KOFF KOFF
PUFF
UFF
HEH... BOTH OF US...
I TOLD YOU IF YOU DIDN'T TAKE A BREAK YOU'D WEAR YOURSELF OUT, YOU DOPE.
WE MADE IT TO THE TOP OF THE TREE.
GOOD!
NARUTO, SASUKE, STARTING TOMORROW...
...YOU TWO CAN HELP SAKURA PROTECT MR. TAZUNA.
YES, SIR!!

WHEW!... WELL, I'M DIRTY, SWEATY, AND REAL WORN OUT FROM ALL OF THE WORK ON THE BRIDGE TODAY...

BUT CONSTRUCTION IS ALMOST COMPLETE!

FATHER, YOU AND NARUTO ARE TWO OF A KIND. PLEASE DON'T WORK YOURSELVES TO DEATH!

OOOHH!

FLOP

YEP.

IF SOMETHING IS PRECIOUS TO YOU...
...PROTECT IT WITH ALL THE STRENGTH YOU'VE GOT!

...INARI...
DON'T CRY...

!

WHY...
WHY...

WHAT'S WRONG?

WHY DO YOU WEAR YOURSELF OUT TRYING?
NO MATTER HOW HARD YOU TRAIN, YOU'LL NEVER BE A MATCH FOR GATÔ'S THUGS!
YOU ACT ALL COOL, AND YOU TALK ALL TOUGH...
...BUT BIG, STRONG GUYS LIKE THAT ARE ALWAYS TOO MUCH FOR PEOPLE WEAKER THAN THEY ARE. THEY'LL DESTROY YOU!!
SLAM!

READ THIS WAY

...
...
...
...

SHUT UP! I'M NOT YOU, AND I'M NOT GONNA LOSE!

JUST WATCHING YOU TICKS ME OFF!

YOU GO RUNNING YOUR MOUTH WHEN YOU DON'T KNOW A THING! THIS ISN'T YOUR TOWN!

AND YOU DON'T KNOW A THING ABOUT ME.
YOU'RE ALWAYS CLOWNING AROUND AND HAVING FUN. YOU DON'T KNOW A THING ABOUT SUFFERING OR LONELINESS OR WHAT MY LIFE IS LIKE!

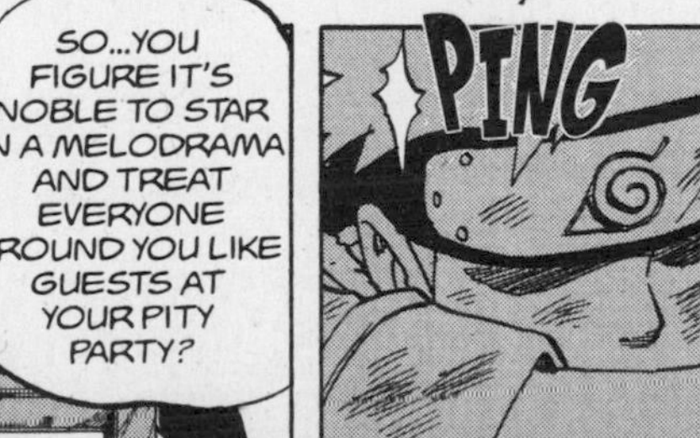

PING

SO...YOU FIGURE IT'S NOBLE TO STAR IN A MELODRAMA AND TREAT EVERYONE AROUND YOU LIKE GUESTS AT YOUR PITY PARTY?
SHFF
!

IT TAKES A REALLY BIG MAN TO SIT AROUND AND CRY... YOU BRAT!
GRRRR
YOU BIG BABY!!
SOB
...

READ
THIS
WAY

...

NARUTO! YOU WENT TOO FAR!
SLAM
SKUFF
HMMF

...

SPLASH
SPLASH

MAY I JOIN YOU...?

YOU KNOW, NARUTO'S KIND OF A BRAT, BUT HE WASN'T TRYING TO BE MEAN OR HATEFUL...
HE JUST... LACKS FINESSE...

...

MR. TAZUNA TOLD US ABOUT WHAT HAPPENED TO YOUR FATHER.

NARUTO GREW UP WITHOUT A FATHER, SAME AS YOU.
jab

...ACTUALLY, WITHOUT ANY PARENTS. HE DOESN'T REMEMBER EITHER ONE OF THEM. OR HAVE A SINGLE FRIEND.
HIS WHOLE LIFE IS ONE BIG, PAINFUL MEMORY.
R-REALLY?

AND IN ALL THE TIME I'VE KNOWN HIM, I'VE NEVER SEEN HIM CRY. OR USE HIS TROUBLES AS AN EXCUSE TO SULK OR BE A COWARD. NOT ONCE.
HE ALWAYS...

READ THIS WAY

I'M OUTTA HERE!

...

STOMP STOMP STOMP STOMPITTY STOMP

ARE YOU READY TO ATTACK?!

TIME TO GO, HAKU.
OF COURSE.
ZABUZA, PAY ATTENTION!!!
ZZT KRACKLE

HEY! HELLO?! WHERE'D EVERYBODY GO?
OH! NARUTO, WHAT ARE YOU DOING UP?

WHAT TH--?!
I OVER-SLEPT--!!

FLUP
OOOH--! I KNEW IT!
FIRST CHANCE THEY GET, THEY LEAVE ME BEHIND!!

STOMP
MASTER KAKASHI WANTED YOU TO TAKE TODAY OFF.
STOMP

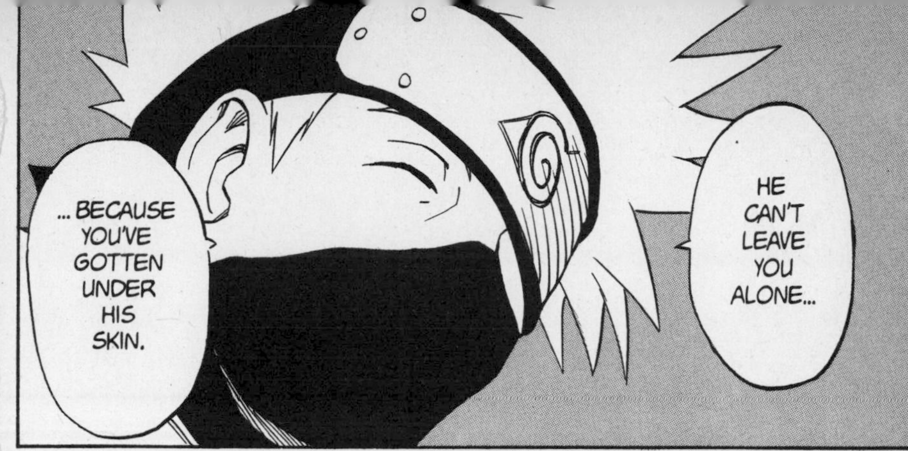
HE CAN'T LEAVE YOU ALONE...
... BECAUSE YOU'VE GOTTEN UNDER HIS SKIN.

...

WELL! PLEASE TAKE CARE OF NARUTO.

HE'S WORN HIMSELF OUT. I DOUBT HE'LL BE ABLE TO MOVE FOR THE REST OF THE DAY.
ZZZZZ
ZZZZZ

WE'RE OFF, TSUNAMI.
BYE.

...TRIES HIS HARDEST, HOPING SOMEONE WILL NOTICE AND GIVE HIM A KIND WORD OR A PAT ON THE BACK.
THAT'S HIS DREAM, AND HE'S RISKED HIS LIFE FOR IT.

I THINK ONE DAY HE MUST HAVE JUST GOTTEN FED UP WITH CRYING.

HE UNDER-STANDS WHAT IT MEANS TO BE STRONG. HE KNOWS WHAT IT COSTS AND WHAT IT'S WORTH...
...JUST AS YOUR FATHER DID.

NARUTO PROBABLY UNDERSTANDS YOU AND KNOWS HOW YOU FEEL BETTER THAN ANY OF THE REST OF US.
WHAT?

OWNG

WH-
WHAT
THE
HELL...?

...
IT CAN'T BE...

M-MONSTERS...

WHAT HAPPENED?!
WHAT... COULD HAVE...?!

INARI-COULD YOU PLEASE HELP ME DO THE LAUNDRY?
TAK
OKAY, MOM-BUT I'M IN THE BATHROOM NOW!!
HEH
K-CHAK

!

THE MIST...

THEY'RE COMING!!

!

!

READ THIS WAY

I WAS RIGHT! HE SURVIVED...
...AND HE'S COME BACK TO FINISH THINGS.

MASTER KAKASHI, IS THIS...?
THAT MAN WE MET...HIS "HIDING IN THE MIST" TECHNIQUE... ISN'T IT?

TOK

SHUDDER

BEEN A WHILE, KAKASHI...

AND I SEE YOU'VE GOT THOSE BRATS TAGGING ALONG, JUST LIKE LAST TIME. AND THE LITTLE BOY IS TREMBLING AGAIN, POOR THING....

I'M SHAKING WITH EAGERNESS FOR A REMATCH!
!!

HAH

GO AHEAD...
...SASUKE.

SWOOSH
TAK

SPLAT

!

DRIP

DRIP

SHHH

WELL! MY WATER DOPPEL-GANGERS WERE OBVIOUSLY NO MATCH FOR YOU!
!
IT SEEMS THE BRATS HAVE MATURED QUITE A BIT...

...INTO WORTHY RIVALS... EH, HAKU?

INDEED!

IT SEEMS THE BRAT HAS MATURED INTO A WORTHY RIVAL... EH, HAKU?
INDEED!

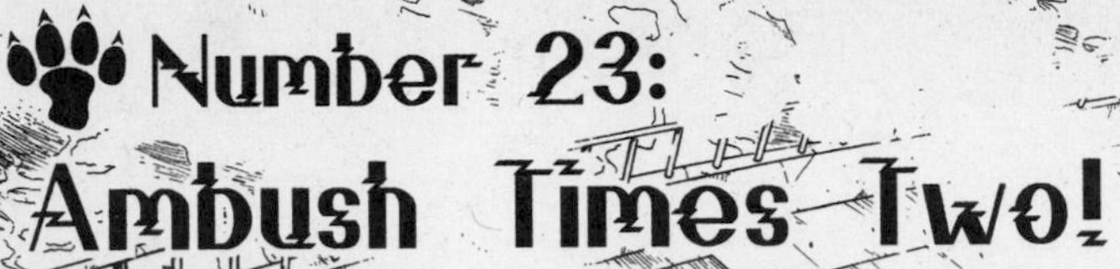

Number 23: Ambush Times Two!

LOOKS LIKE I WAS RIGHT.

OH!

OUR MYSTERIOUS MASKED FRIEND...
... IS PLAYING ON ZABUZA'S TEAM.
HE HAS NERVE, SHOWING UP LIKE THIS!
THIS ONE'S MINE.
EH...?
IMPRESSIVE KID, ISN'T HE?
EVEN IF YOUR WATER DOPPELGANGERS HAVE ONLY A TENTH OF THE STRENGTH OF THE ORIGINALS...
SAKURA CHALLENGES EVERYTHING NARUTO SAYS OR DOES... BUT SHE TAKES SASUKE COMPLETELY AT FACE VALUE, WITHOUT QUESTION.
SASUKE'S SO COOL!! ♡
THAT WAS QUITE A SHOW YOU PUT ON BEFORE,
BUT WE'RE ON TO YOU NOW... AND I HATE HAM ACTORS!

...IT'S AMAZING HE WAS ABLE TO DO SO WELL.
BUT WE'RE STILL ON THE OFFENSIVE.
GO!
YES, SIR.
TAK
!!
WHAT?!
SHF
!!

TAK
!
TAK

OLD MAN TAZUNA'S DAUGHTER, HUH?
SORRY, BUT YOU'RE COMING WITH US.

SPLASH

CRASH
!!
AIEE...!!

MAMA!!
WHAT DO YOU WANT, BRAT?!
!

RUN, INARI! DON'T COME IN!!!

SHOULD WE GRAB HIM, TOO?
WE ONLY NEED ONE HOSTAGE.

READ THIS WAY

FLINCH
HOSTAGE...?!

HEH-HEH... TOO BAD --
-- FOR HIM!
KLAT

!!
SHIVER

WAIT!!

...IF YOU DARE TOUCH MY CHILD... I'LL BITE THROUGH MY TONGUE AND DROWN IN MY OWN BLOOD.

THEN WHAT WILL YOU DO FOR A LIVE HOSTAGE?

READ THIS WAY

HEH... BE GRATEFUL TO YOUR MA, KIDDO.
AW, MAN... BUT I'M DYIN' TO CUT SOMEONE!

RELAX. YOU GAVE YOUR BLADE A PRETTY GOOD WORKOUT BEFORE WE EVEN GOT HERE.
SO GET OVER IT, AND LET'S GO.
SOB
SOB
SOB

MAMA... I'M SO SORRY...
I'M A WEAK LITTLE CRYBABY... I CAN'T SAVE YOU...

AND I'M AFRAID!
I DON'T WANT TO DIE!

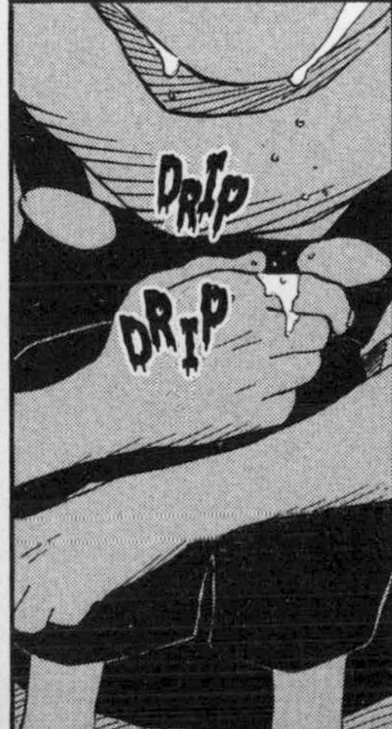

DRIP
DRIP

YOU BIG BABY!!

I THINK ONE DAY HE MUST HAVE JUST GOTTEN FED UP WITH CRYING.

YOU FIGURE IT'S NOBLE TO STAR IN A MELODRAMA AND TREAT EVERYONE AROUND YOU LIKE GUESTS AT YOUR PITY PARTY?
...

HE UNDERSTANDS WHAT IT MEANS TO BE STRONG. HE KNOWS WHAT IT COSTS AND WHAT IT'S WORTH...
...JUST AS YOUR FATHER DID.

...

IT TAKES A REALLY BIG MAN TO SIT AROUND AND CRY... YOU BRAT!
YOU BIG BABY!!!!

IF SOMETHING IS PRECIOUS TO YOU...
...PROTECT IT WITH ALL THE STRENGTH YOU'VE GOT...
...EVEN AT THE RISK OF YOUR OWN LIFE!

EVERYONE ELSE IS... SO AWESOME...

SO COOL...

...AND STRONG...

CLENCH
FAN!

COULD I...
BE STRONG TOO...
...CAN I...
...DADDY?!

HEH-HEH... SUCH BEAUTIFUL SKIN. SO SMOOTH AND LOVELY. IT'S A SHAME NOT TO BE ABLE TO CUT IT...
STOP DAWD-LING!

WAIT!!
STAMP

!
HUH?

INARI!!
WELL, LOOKY THERE. THE BRAT CAME BACK.

Y...
YES, I CAN...!!
YOU GET AWAY FROM MY MAMA--!!

RRRR RROAR!!
TAK TAK
!
JEEZ, THIS KID IS A WASTE OF SPACE!!

!
SO CUT HIM...
YEAH...!
KLAT

INARI!

!

!

SNK

SORRY I'M LATE.

!

THUNK

THE ART OF SUBSTITUTION...!?

WAY TO GO, INARI!!!

N-NARUTO...!

IT'S BEING A HERO, Y'KNOW? ALL THAT NICK OF TIME STUFF!

NARUTO! WILL YOU BE OKAY?
TAK
TAK

TAK
HEY! ISN'T THAT...
ONE OF TAZUNA'S CUT-RATE BODY-GUARDS?!
WHEN YOU DISTRACTED THEM, I WAS ABLE TO SAVE YOUR MOTHER!

HAH! YOU EXPECT THOSE TOYS TO AFFECT US?
PING
PING

SHINNG
SHINNNG

NO SWEAT.
KLIK

SUCKERS!

POW

NARUTO... HOW'D YOU KNOW THOSE SAMURAI WERE COMING?
HUNH--?

THERE WAS A STUCK PIG BACK IN THE FOREST, CUT TO RIBBONS WITH A SWORD...
...AND TREES WITH FRESH DEEP SLASHES IN THEIR BARK, GOING IN THE DIRECTION OF YOUR HOUSE. WASN'T TOO HARD TO FIGURE OUT... I GOT WORRIED.
!

BUT FORGET THAT...

INARI... I OWE YOU AN APOLOGY.
!

WHY?

WELL, UMMM...

I'M SORRY I CALLED YOU A BABY.
AND IT'S NOT TRUE. OKAY?

BAP
!

YOU'RE A BIG, STRONG BOY--!

...

OHHH... OH NO...!
?

...I PROMISED MYSELF I WOULDN'T CRY...
NOW YOU'LL MAKE FUN OF ME AGAIN...

READ THIS WAY

HUH?

...
NO WAY!!

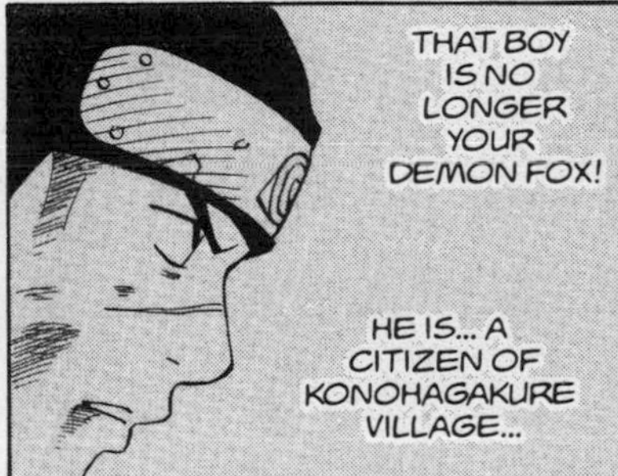

THAT BOY IS NO LONGER YOUR DEMON FOX!
HE IS... A CITIZEN OF KONOHAGAKURE VILLAGE...

...FOR HIM, I HAVE NOTHING BUT RESPECT.
HE'S AN EXCELLENT STUDENT.

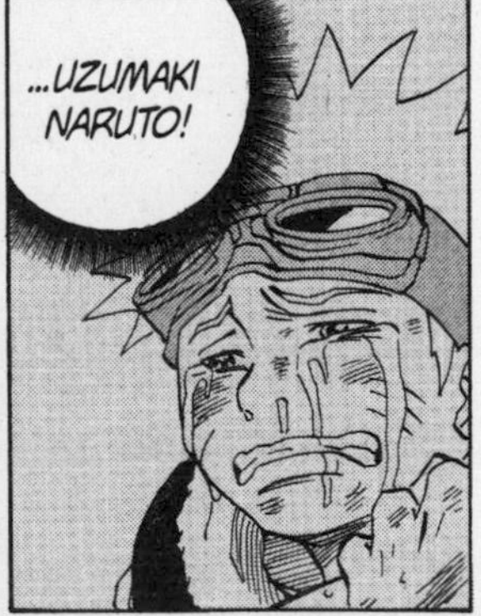

...UZUMAKI NARUTO!

...

?

NOTHING WRONG WITH CRYING...

...WHEN YOU'RE HAPPY!

IF THEY ATTACKED US HERE, IT MEANS THE BRIDGE IS PROBABLY A TARGET, TOO!

SO-

WOW!
NARUTO ...I WISH YOU WERE MY BIG BROTHER...

YEAH...
...
WIPE
WIPE

YOU CAN HANDLE THINGS HERE, RIGHT?

MAN, THIS "HERO" THING IS A LOT OF WORK!!
SWIPE
YOU BET!
CLENCH

WITH JUST ONE HAND, HE'S...!!

WHAT?!!

HE'S MAKING SIGNS WITH JUST ONE HAND?! I'VE NEVER SEEN ANYTHING LIKE IT...

FWUP

FWUP

FWUP

STAMP
STAMP

SECRET ART OF WATER!
THE THOUSAND STINGING NEEDLES OF DEATH!

ZIPP

ZIPP

ZIPP

!

I DON'T WANT TO HAVE TO KILL YOU, BUT...
YOU PROBABLY WON'T LEAVE QUIETLY, WILL YOU?...

DON'T BE STUPID...

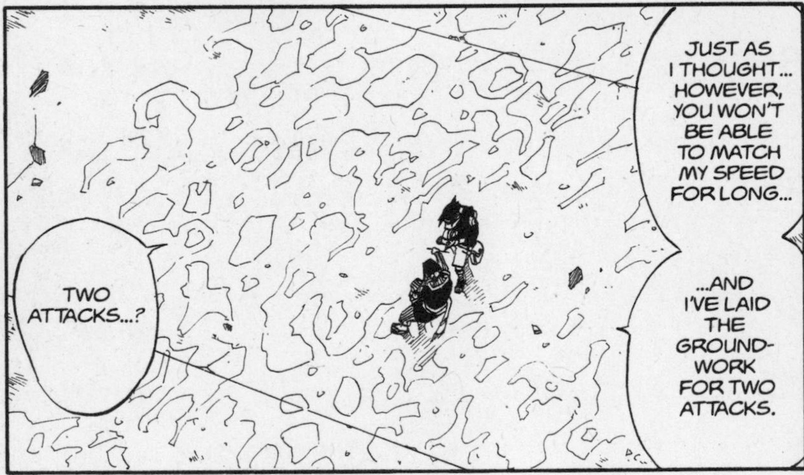
JUST AS I THOUGHT... HOWEVER, YOU WON'T BE ABLE TO MATCH MY SPEED FOR LONG...
...AND I'VE LAID THE GROUND-WORK FOR TWO ATTACKS.
TWO ATTACKS...?

FIRSTLY, THERE'S THE WATER SPLASHED ALL AROUND US. SECONDLY, I'VE TRAPPED ONE OF YOUR HANDS WITH PARRYING THIS MOVE...
KREE
KREE
...WHICH LEAVES YOU ONLY ONE HAND FREE TO DEFEND YOURSELF FROM MY ATTACKS!

READ THIS WAY

AHA...
HE CAN KEEP UP WITH HAKU'S SPEED.

SAKURA! WE HAVE TO COVER MR. TAZUNA. TAKE THAT SIDE, AND STAY CLOSE!
LET SASUKE HANDLE HAKU.
YES, SIR!
SPLAT
TAK

Number 24: Speed!!

READ THIS WAY

SO... "I DON'T WANT TO HAVE TO KILL YOU"...?
I WONDER IF HE TRULY MEANS THAT!
SIGH

SASUKE!!

!

COME ON!
GOTTA REMEMBER THE TRAINING!

SUMMON ALL OF THE CHAKRA ENERGY YOU CAN...

...AND FOCUS IT IN MY FEET!!

SPLATTER

HOP!

!
THUK THUK THUK
CHINNNG!
SPLASH
THOK
HOP
!!
YOU'RE NOT THAT FAST.
NOW YOU'RE THE ONE WHO HAS TO WORRY...
...ABOUT DEFENDING YOURSELF FROM MY ATTACKS.

SWIPE
KASHING
SLASH
!

SWUP
FLIP
!
...H... HE'S FAST...!!
WHU

POW
WHAT...?!
HAKU... IS ACTUALLY LOSING A BATTLE OF SPEED?!
YOU'RE FAST. I'M FASTER.
SKID
UHN!
YOU HAD THAT COMING... FOR UNDER-ESTIMATING MY TEAM... AND FOR NAME-CALLING.
HE MAY NOT LOOK LIKE MUCH... BUT SASUKE HERE IS THE TOP-RATED ROOKIE FROM ALL OF KONOHAGAKURE VILLAGE.
AND SAKURA HERE IS OUR SHARPEST MIND...
THAT'S FOR SURE!
INNER SAKURA
OH, YESS!
OH
AND LAST BUT NOT LEAST...
...LET'S NOT FORGET OUR OWN COMEDY NINJA - THE MAVERICK SHOW-STOPPER, THE ONE AND ONLY NARUTO!
AH-CHOO!

HEH
HEH
HEH...
HEH
HEH
HEH
HEH...

?

HAKU...
DO YOU
UNDERSTAND,
IF THIS GOES
ON, YOU COULD
END UP DYING
AT THE HANDS
OF THE VERY
PERSON YOU
SOUGHT TO
SPARE?

YES,
I
DO...
WHAT
A
PITY.
WH...
WHY...
....DOES
THE AIR
SUDDENLY
FEEL SO...
COLD?

RISE

!
PLIT
SPLISH
KRINKLE

SECRET ART OF WATER...

CLINK
ICE CRYSTAL MAGIC MIRROR TECHNIQUE!

READ THIS WAY

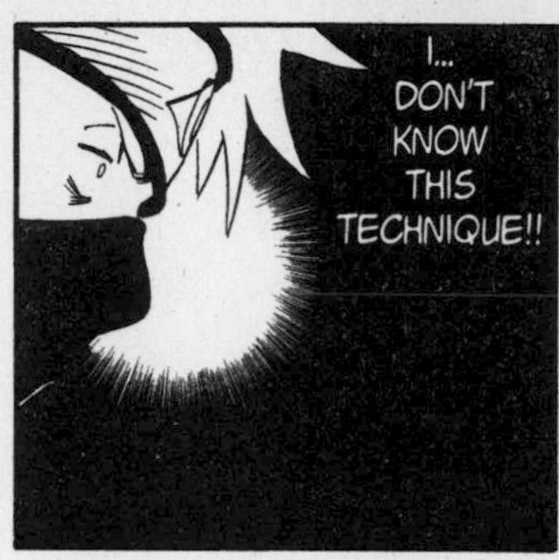
I... DON'T KNOW THIS TECHNIQUE!!

GLEAM

SPLASH

SLUUUUP

!
WHA...?

CLINT
SHM
POP

!
POP
POP
POP
POP
POP
POP

READ THIS WAY

BLAST!
HOP

POP
!

LET'S NOT FORGET...
I'M YOUR ENEMY.

OUR CHILDREN CAN PLAY TOGETHER... WHILE MY BOY KILLS YOURS.
NO...

NOW THAT IT'S ALL IN PLACE...
WHAT'S HE PLANNING TO DO WITH THESE MIRRORS?
...LET ME SHOW YOU SOME REAL SPEED!

!
OWW!!!

GRAB

SLASH
SLASH
SLASH
AUUGH!!
SLASH
SLASH
SLASH

SASUKE...!!

AAAARGH--!!
ANY SUDDEN MOVES AND I'LL KILL THOSE OTHER TWO!!
YOU...!!
SASUKE!!
GGH- GYAAGGH!
!!
...
MR. TAZUNA, I'M SORRY... BUT I'M GOING TO HAVE TO LEAVE YOU FOR JUST A LITTLE BIT.
GO AHEAD.
I'LL BE FINE!
TAK!
KLAP
SASUKE!!

POP
GRAB

!!
!
!!
HE CAUGHT IT!!

!
...WHO...?
OOONNN
THAT IDIOT...
...SHOW-OFF...
...THE MAVERICK SHOW-STOPPER...
COMEDY NINJA...?!
UZUMAKI NARUTO!
AT YOUR SERVICE!!

HARUNO SAKURA

EARLY CHARACTER DESIGNS

This was how I first imagined Sakura. Let's face it...she's really not that cute, is she? Especially back then! But that was mostly because I'm not that good with female characters in general, so making one of them cute is always a big challenge for me.

When my editor, those around me, and even my own staff saw this design and read her personality profile, they all assured me that Sakura was "far from cute"! Heh-heh...

But I have my own reasons for being especially fond of Sakura, both in how she's designed, and in her personality. I believe everyone possesses an "Inner Sakura" type voice in their heart, including things like her entirely arbitrary choice of love object. I think it gives her a real humanity that's pretty sweet.

There's a lot more to being a good female manga character than just cuteness, you know....At least, that's my excuse. The troublemakers and the curmudgeons I can draw without breaking a sweat... but girls are really hard!

Number 25: For Your Dreams...!!

YOU KNOW HOW THE STORY GOES. THINGS LOOK BLEAK... TILL THE HERO ARRIVES --

HERE I AM, TO SAVE THE DAY.

AND THEN - **POW!!** - BYE-BYE BAD GUYS!

WHAT WE NEEDED WAS AN AMBUSH. INSTEAD, HE ALL BUT PAINTS A TARGET ON HIMSELF!

EXASPERATING LITTLE --!

...

THE BRAT AGAIN, HUNH?
HMPH

BIG TALKER...

NARUTO!

READ THIS WAY
TRAINING!!
TO BUILD UP MY STRENGTH!
HEH
!
BLAST!
FWUP
FWIP
FWIP
!
HERE IT COMES!!
FWIP
FWIP
FWIP
SHF

CHING
CHING
CHING
!
CHING
CHING

READ
THIS
WAY

SO, YOU WANT ME TO KEEP MY HANDS OFF HIM, EH, HAKU?
HOW CHARMINGLY NAÏVE OF YOU... AS USUAL...

...

THAT GUY... NAÏVE? YEAH, RIGHT!
LOOK AT ME... IT'S LIKE I'M BEING CUT TO RIBBONS BY A THOUSAND NEEDLES...
...BUT THE CUTS ARE ALL SUPERFICIAL. HE'S KILLING ME BY INCHES... SAVING THE VITAL TARGETS, AND THE DEATHBLOW, FOR LATER.

BUT I CAN'T FIGURE OUT WHAT TECHNIQUE HE'S USING! HIS DOPPEL-GANGERS ALL HIDE WITHIN THE MIRRORS AND THEN STRIKE SIMULTANEOUSLY!
I DON'T EVEN SEE HIM MOVE. HE STRIKES BEFORE I CAN SPOT HIS WEAPONS' TRAJECTORY!

IT CAN'T JUST BE THE ART OF THE DOPPEL-GANGER... THE ICE MIRRORS ARE A PART OF THIS, SOMEHOW, BUT I CAN'T FIGURE OUT THEIR SIGNIFICANCE!
WHATEVER IS GOING ON, THE MIRRORS MUST BE THE KEY!

LOOKS LIKE MY ONLY CHANCE IS TO CONCENTRATE ON THE BATTLE HERE!...
AND TRUST NARUTO TO SET ME FREE FROM OUTSIDE....

TA-DAA!!

YO! SASUKE! I'M HERE TO RESCUE YOU!

FLIP

!!!

Y-YOU DOOFUS! NO STEALTH... NO CAUTION... AND YOU CALL YOURSELF A NINJA?!
NOW THAT YOU'VE GOTTEN YOURSELF TRAPPED IN HERE WITH ME... JUST DO WHAT YOU WANT. I DON'T REALLY CARE.
OH, FINE!!! I WENT THROUGH HELL TO RESCUE YOU, AND THIS IS THE THANKS I GET?!

LEAVE IT TO THE TEAM MAVERICK.
ONCE HE STARTS "HELPING"... THINGS GO FROM BAD TO WORSE!

...IF I GO TO HELP NARUTO AND SASUKE, MR. TAZUNA WILL BE COMPLETELY EXPOSED...
...BUT I CAN'T JUST ABANDON THE BOYS!

BUT AT THE FIRST SIGN OF A SHADOW DOPPELGANGER FROM ME...
HE'LL COUNTER WITH HIS WATER DOPPELGANGERS... I'D JUST BE SQUANDERING MY CHAKRAS...

SHLUK

SHLOOP
!
!

SO THAT'S IT! HIS REAL BODY IS OVER THERE!
POK

!!
OVER HERE.

HUNH?

LOOKS LIKE...
DESTROYING ALL THE MIRRORS MAY BE OUR ONLY HOPE!
WH-WHAT THE HELL IS GOING ON!!
BAM

FIRE STYLE!
THESE ARE MIRRORS MADE OF ICE, SO...

FLAR

BLAZE OF GLORY!!!

UGH...
THAT PITIFUL FLAME WILL BARELY TOUCH MY ICE MIRRORS...
IT'S NOT EVEN MAKING A DENT!!!

ROARR

GLEA
SHF

GAAH!!
CLOP
AUGH!!

SHR
SHR
SHR

WHERE'S THE ATTACK COMING FROM? ARE THEY ALL DOPPELGANGERS?
WHICH ONE OF YOU IS REAL?!
GRR

YOUR EYES WILL NEVER SEE THE TRUTH.
I CAN'T BE CAUGHT.

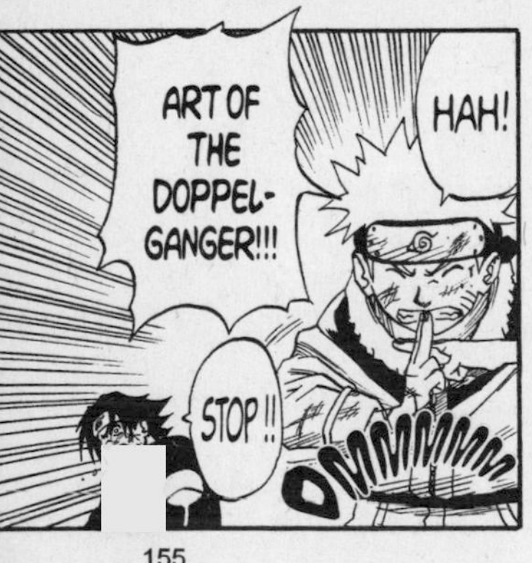
HAH!
ART OF THE DOPPEL-GANGER!!!
STOP!!

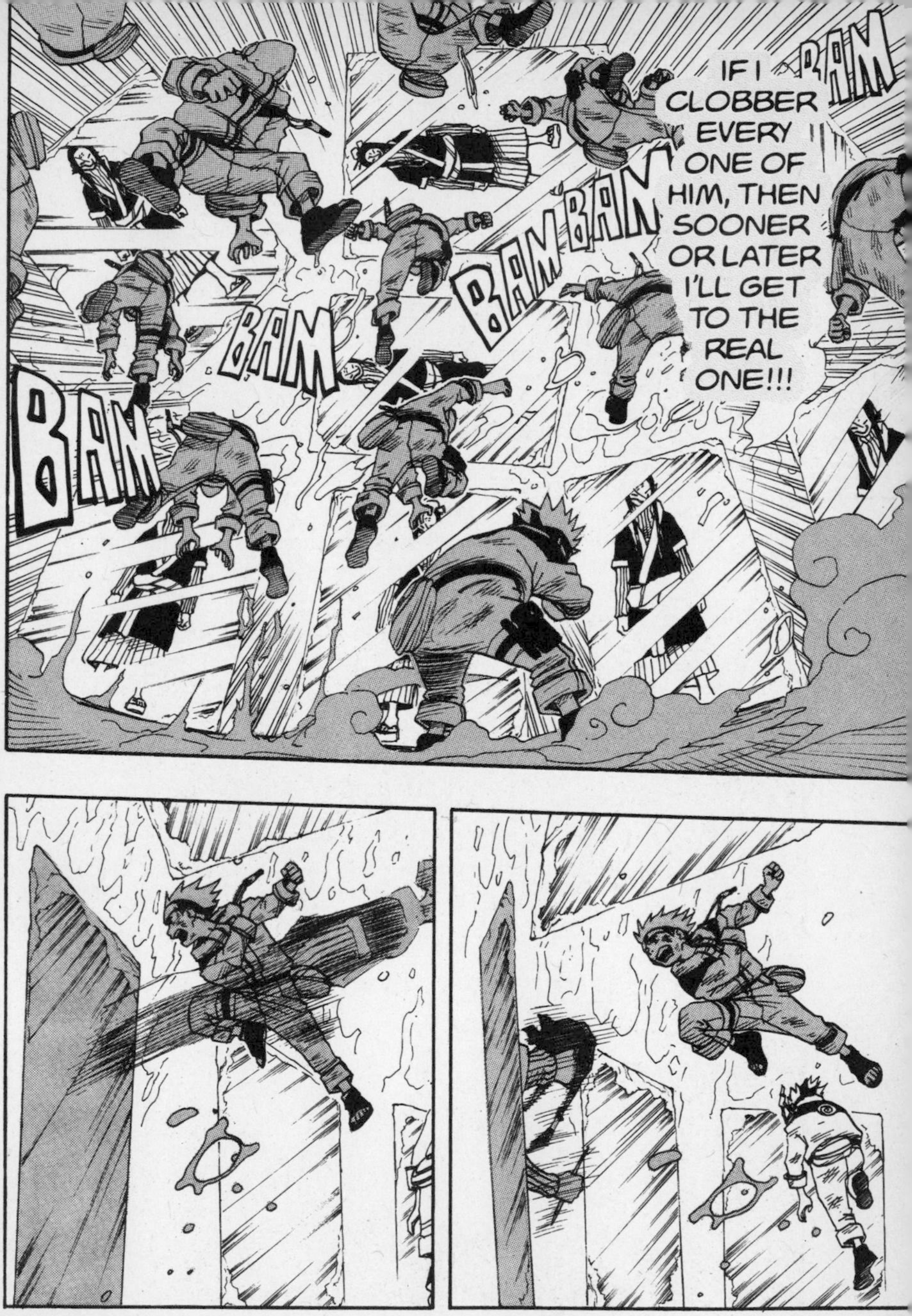

IF I CLOBBER EVERY ONE OF HIM, THEN SOONER OR LATER I'LL GET TO THE REAL ONE!!!

BAM BAM BAM BAM BAM BAM

CRLAK

SHF

AUGH!!!!
POW
POW
POW
POW
POW
POW
!

SKIIIIID

THE TECHNIQUE I'M USING IS PART OF THE ART OF TELEPORTATION, AND THE ONLY TOOL I NEED TO PERFORM IT IS THE MIRRORS THAT HOLD MY IMAGE.
I MOVE SO QUICKLY, THE PAIR OF YOU MIGHT AS WELL BE STANDING STILL!

!
SO THAT'S IT!!!

I NEVER IMAGINED THAT ANYONE COULD MASTER SUCH A TECHNIQUE AT SO YOUNG AN AGE!
HEH HEH HEH HEH...

!
"SUCH A TECH-NIQUE"...?

IT'S A KEKKEI GENKAI— A SKILL THAT CAN BE PASSED FROM ONE GENERATION TO THE NEXT!

YOU MEAN...

A **GENETIC** TRAIT... RUNNING THROUGH THE BLOODLINES OF THOSE OF THE PUREST SHINOBI PEDIGREE...
SOME OF THE MOST EXTRAORDINARY TECHNIQUES ARE HANDED DOWN FROM GENERATION TO GENERATION SOLELY ON THAT BASIS...

PRECISELY... IT'S OF THE SAME ORDER OF SKILL AS MY SHARINGAN MIRROR EYE....
BUT EVEN MY SHARINGAN CAN'T COPY, MIMIC, OR BREAK THIS BOY'S *KEKKEI GENKAI!*

...
I'VE HAD ENOUGH...

SO, IS THIS IT?
!

IT CAN'T END LIKE THIS!
I'VE GOT A DREAM TO FULFILL!

TO BECOME TOP DOG IN MY HOME TOWN!
ALL THE PEOPLE WHO USED TO TREAT ME LIKE DIRT WILL HAVE TO SAY "HE'S THE NUMBER ONE NINJA"!

DREAMS...

PATHETIC!

LOOK AT YOU... A FOUNDLING. AN ORPHAN. THROWN AWAY. UNLOVED AND UNCARED FOR...

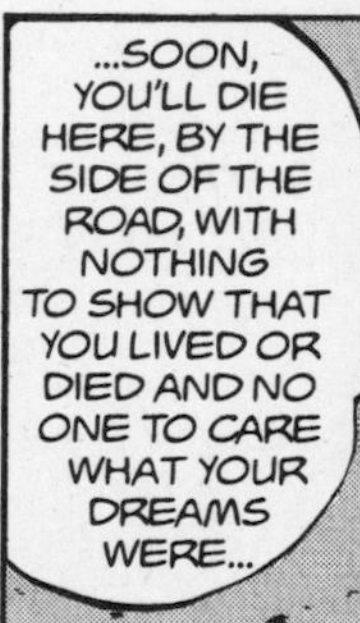
...SOON, YOU'LL DIE HERE, BY THE SIDE OF THE ROAD, WITH NOTHING TO SHOW THAT YOU LIVED OR DIED AND NO ONE TO CARE WHAT YOUR DREAMS WERE...

!

...I... CAN SEE MYSELF IN YOUR EYES. WE HAVE THE SAME EXPRESSION!

I...
FIND IT DIFFICULT TO EMBRACE THE FULL SHINOBI PHILOSOPHY.

...

I CAN'T HELP BUT PREFER THAT THE PAIR OF YOU...
... NOT FORCE ME TO KILL YOU.

HOWEVER, IF YOU TWO ARE GOING TO COME AT ME...
I SHALL KILL MY OWN HEART WITH MY BLADE– JUST AS THE WORD "SHINOBI" WAS ORIGINALLY THE WORDS "HEART" AND "BLADE"– AND ACT AS A FULL-FLEDGED SHINOBI WOULD!

THIS BRIDGE IS A NEXUS OF OUR DESTINIES...
... AND ALL OF OUR DREAMS AND FUTURES BALANCE ON THE EDGE OF A KNIFE.

I HAVE MY OWN DREAMS....

...AS YOU HAVE YOURS...

PLEASE TRY NOT TO RESENT ME, BUT I'M WILLING TO DO WHATEVER IT TAKES...

...TO PROTECT THE ONE I CARE ABOUT MOST.... TO FIGHT, KILL, OR DIE TO FULFILL THAT PERSON'S DREAMS.
DOING SO IS MY OWN DREAM.

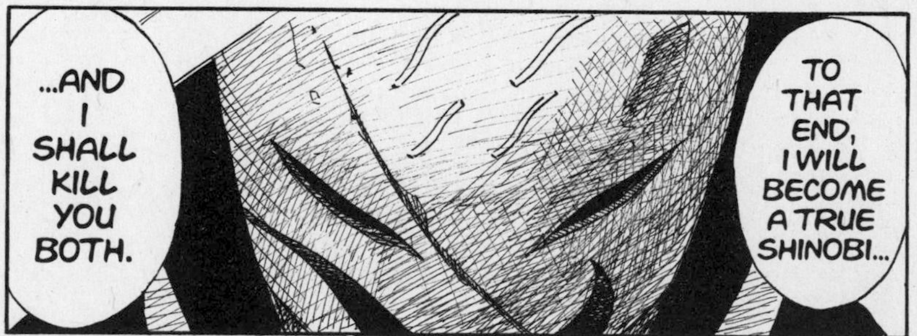
TO THAT END, I WILL BECOME A TRUE SHINOBI...
...AND I SHALL KILL YOU BOTH.

SASUKE! NARUTO! DON'T YOU DARE LOSE TO A PERSON LIKE HIM!!!!

STOP ENCOURAGING THEM, SAKURA!!
HUNH?

EVEN IF WE KNEW OF A WAY TO COUNTER HIS TECHNIQUE, YOUR TEAMMATES STILL WOULDN'T BE UP TO THE TASK OF DEFEATING THAT BOY.

!
WH-WHAT DO YOU MEAN?

HEH HEH...
HEH HEH HEH...

THOSE TWO HAVEN'T YET DEVELOPED THE PSYCHOLOGICAL STRENGTH...
TO TURN THEIR HEARTS TO ICE AND TAKE A HUMAN LIFE.

NO TRUE SHINOBI COULD EVER BE BORN OF A A PLACE LIKE YOUR VILLAGE, A PLACE OF WEAKNESS... OF PEACE.
YOU DON'T LIVE WITH DEATH, OR GROW UP NEEDING TO KILL TO ENSURE YOUR OWN SURVIVAL. IN YOU THOSE SKILLS--AND THE MINDSET THEY REQUIRE--DIE STILLBORN!

THAT BOY HAS LIVED WITH THE KIND OF EMOTIONAL ANGUISH THAT PREPARES HIM TO BE A TRUE SHINOBI.

MASTER KAKASHI... WHAT CAN WE DO?

...

SHA

YOU'LL FORGIVE ME...
... IF I PUT AN END TO THIS...!

Number 26:
Sharingan Devastation!!

SHA

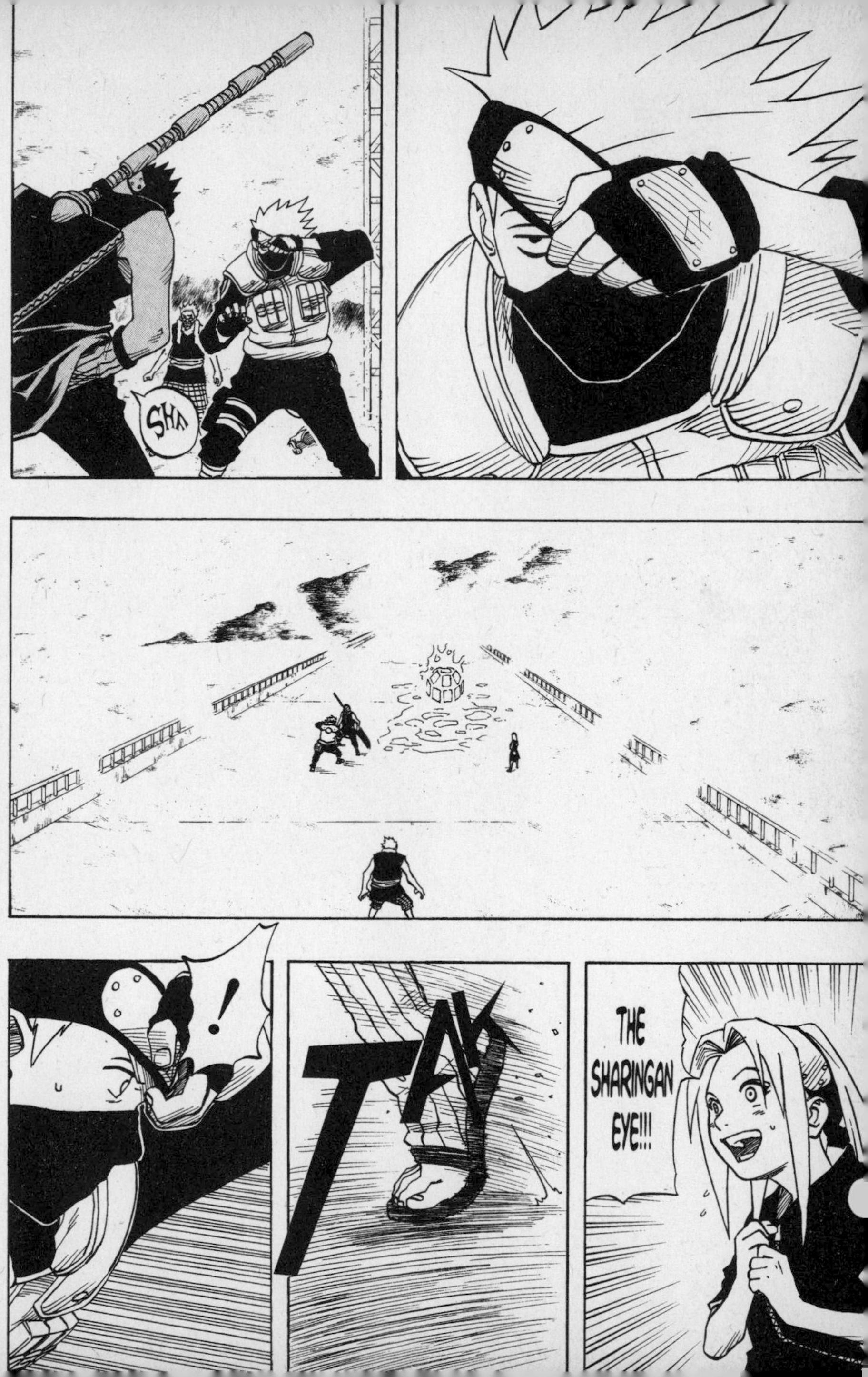

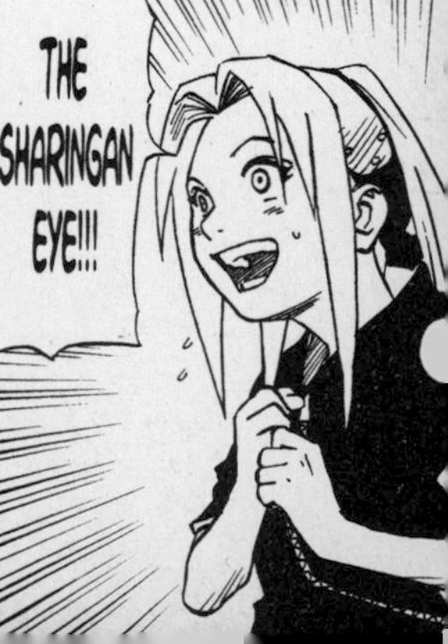
THE SHARINGAN EYE!!!

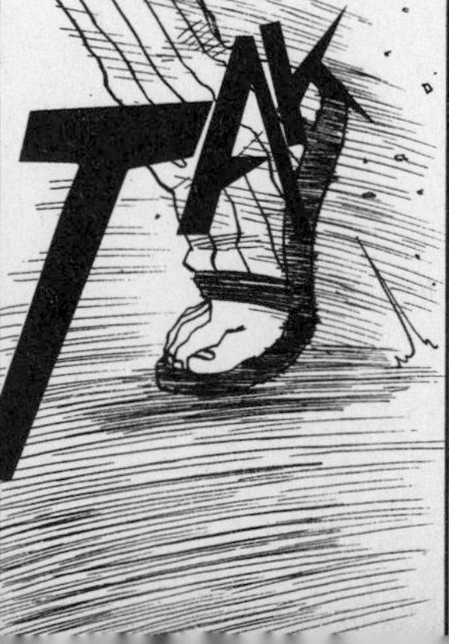
TAK

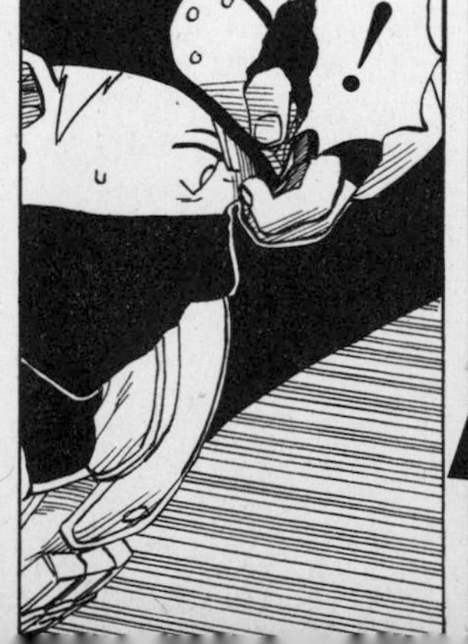
!

SHING
SHUNK
PLIT
PLIT
PLIT

YOU CAN SNEER ALL YOU WANT ABOUT MY "LACK OF FINESSE," ZABUZA... IT DOESN'T CHANGE THE FACT THAT YOU'RE AFRAID OF THE SHARINGAN. AND OF ME.

HEH HEH HEH... A NINJA'S SECRET WEAPON...
... SHOULD BE EMPLOYED JUDICIOUSLY, NOT DISPLAYED AT RANDOM TO EVERY FOE YOU FACE!
HEH

YOU SHOULD FEEL PRIVILEGED. NO ONE ELSE HAS EVER LIVED TO SEE THE SHARINGAN A SECOND TIME.
AND NO ONE WILL EVER SEE IT THRICE!
HEH HEH... BY ALL MEANS, DEFEAT ME, IF YOU CAN. YOU STILL WON'T HAVE WHAT IT TAKES TO KILL HAKU!

THAT MASKED BOY IS SO POWERFUL, EVEN MASTER KAKASHI CAN'T WIN...?!
MASTER...!

SINCE HE WAS A TODDLER...
... I'VE BEATEN HIS FIGHTING SKILLS INTO HIM!

EVEN IN THE FACE OF UNTHINK-ABLE ADVERSITY, HE HAS ALWAYS PREVAILED!
HE'S LOST ALL REGARD FOR HIS OWN LIFE AND BECOME A KILLING MACHINE... A TRUE SHINOBI.

HIS SKILLS SURPASS EVEN MY OWN.
AND HE BEARS WITHIN HIM THE FORMIDABLE LEGACY OF AN INHERITED *KEKKEI GENKAI!*

SHLUPP
THUS, I HAVE FORGED AND CARRY WITH ME A WEAPON OF MATCHLESS QUALITY AND SKILL...
... ENTIRELY UNLIKE THE SCRAPS OF TRASH THAT FOLLOW AT YOUR HEELS.

DNNNNG
IS THERE ANYTHING DULLER THAN LISTENING TO SOMEONE ELSE BRAG?
IT'S SHOW TIME!

PERHAPS YOU MIGHT HOLD OFF A MOMENT, NOW THAT I'VE CAUGHT MY BREATH. AND—TO BORROW YOUR OWN IDIOM—PERMIT ME ONE MORE BOAST.
YOU TURNED A VERY PRETTY PHRASE AT OUR LAST ENCOUNTER...

?!

!

FRANKLY, I'VE BEEN DYING TO STEAL IT.
...

?

SOME-THING TO THE EFFECT OF, "JUST SO YOU KNOW"...
..."THE SAME SPELL WON'T WORK ON ME TWICE."
HEH

READ THIS WAY

HAVING HAD A CHANCE TO SEE IT IN ACTION...
...I NOW HAVE A THOROUGH UNDERSTAND-ING OF THE ARCANE WORKINGS OF YOUR MIRROR EYE.

THERE WAS FAR MORE TO OUR PREVIOUS BATTLE THAN THE APPARENTLY HUMILIATING DEFEAT I PERMITTED YOU TO HAND ME.
UHN...!
THAT'S THAT...
HAKU, WHO WAS HIDING NEARBY, OBSERVED AND STUDIED EVERY ASPECT OF OUR FIGHT, FROM BEGINNING TO END.

HAKU IS EXTREMELY INTELLIGENT. FOR HIM, TO SEE A TECHNIQUE IS TO ANALYZE AND UNDERSTAND IT. AND WITH THAT UNDERSTANDING, HE CAN DEVELOP EFFECTIVE COUNTER-MEASURES.
!

* "The Art of Hiding in the Mist"

WE'RE BOTH WOUNDED, BUT WE HAVE TO SUCK IT UP AND GO ON. WE'LL BE FINE AS LONG AS HE DOESN'T KILL ONE OF US!! THERE MUST BE A LIMIT TO HIS CHAKRA. HIS ATTACKS HAVE BEEN GETTING WEAKER!

SHUT UP AND GET ON YOUR FEET! I CAN'T FIGHT HIM AND WATCH OUT FOR YOU, TOO!
SASUKE! WE'VE GOTTA STOP REACTING AND TAKE BACK THE INITIATIVE!!
AW, MAN...

SHUK

TAK

HE'S COMING!!!
CHING

FWUF

...HE'S RIGHT... I'VE GOT TO HAVE FAITH IN SASUKE...
...AND CONCENTRATE ON WHAT I HAVE TO DO.

...

SAKURA! I'M COUNTING ON YOU TO PROTECT MR. TAZUNA!!!
!

WHERE THE HELL IS THIS FOG COMING FROM? YOU CAN'T SEE YOUR HAND IN FRONT OF YOUR FACE!

THE AIR IS CRACKLING WITH HIS ENERGY, MR. TAZUNA!
STAY BY MY SIDE!!
TAK
ALL RIGHT, SAKURA...!

THIS FOG IS TOO THICK FOR THE HIDING-IN-THE-MIST TECHNIQUE!
EVEN ZABUZA WON'T BE ABLE TO SEE ANYTHING THROUGH IT.

VIIIN VIIIN

!

CHING
GASP!
CHING
CHING
CHING
CHING
CHING
CHING

YOU REPELLED THOSE NICELY... NO LESS THAN I'D EXPECT OF KAKASHI OF THE SHARINGAN EYE.
SHH
!

HIS EYES ARE CLOSED!!

HOWEVER... THE NEXT TIME YOU SEE ME... IT WILL STILL BE THE END.

YOU'VE OVERESTIMATED THE VALUE OF YOUR SHARINGAN.
SHM

WHAT...?

SHHH
HEH HEH HEH...

READ THIS WAY

YOU PRETEND IT ENABLES YOU TO PENETRATE ALL... YET...
...CAN YOU SEE THE FUTURE?

I FORESEE... YOUR DEATH.
BUT YOU'VE TURNED OUT TO BE A FALSE PROPHET AFTER ALL, KAKASHI...

YOU CAN NEITHER READ MY MIND NOR THE FUTURE.
IN OTHER WORDS, YOUR PRECIOUS SHARINGAN IS JUST AN ELABORATE HOAX, A CONFIDENCE TRICK YOU PLAY IN ORDER TO PSYCH OUT YOUR OPPONENTS.

MORE PRECISELY, IT COMBINES CLARITY OF PERCEPTION AND INSIGHT ON YOUR OWN PART WITH THE ABILITY TO ALL BUT HYPNOTIZE THOSE AROUND YOU!
USING THOSE SKILLS IN CONCERT, YOU ARE ABLE TO CREATE YOUR ILLUSIONS THROUGH A COMBINATION OF MIMICRY— FROM MOVEMENT, TO THOUGHTS, TO THE SKILLS OF THOSE YOU FIGHT!

PRANCING AROUND ACTING LIKE YOU CAN SEE THE FUTURE!

YOU ANALYZE MY SUPERFICIAL MOVEMENTS, COPY THEM, AND USE THE RAPIDITY OF THE TURNAROUND TO INDUCE FEAR AND INSECURITY.
FWUP
COPYING FORM...
!!!

FEH... YOU'RE A PALE IMITATION.
COPYING THOUGHT...
I'M THE GENUINE ARTICLE. NO MERE COPYCAT STANDS A CHANCE AGAINST ME.
ONCE YOU'RE CERTAIN YOU UNDERSTAND WHAT'S GOING ON IN MY HEART AND MIND, YOU CALCULATE JUST WHAT TO SAY TO BEND MY MIND TO YOUR WILL, AND THEN...
YOU CALCULATE WHEN MY INSECURITIES HAVE REACHED A FEVER PITCH, AND THEN YOU LAY YOUR TRAP.
YOU USE VISUAL HYPNOSIS TO TRICK ME INTO SIGNALLING WHAT TECHNIQUE I'LL USE AND HOW I'LL BE USING IT.
COPYING NINJUTSU...
... AND THEN ALL YOU HAVE TO DO IS MIMIC IT!

!

KNOWING THAT, IT WAS SIMPLE TO CHOOSE A COUNTER-MEASURE.

FIRST, I CONCEAL MYSELF WITHIN THIS THICK MIST AND NEUTRALIZE YOUR VISUAL ACUITY.

UHN!

POW

AAGH...! IT'S HARD TO BLOCK WHAT I CAN'T SEE!!!

SHM SHM SHM

AH--!

HEH HEH... WITH MY OWN EYES CLOSED, I ELIMINATE THE POSSIBILITY OF YOUR HYPNOTIZING ME WHILE WE'RE IN CLOSE PROXIMITY.

SKF SKF SKF

I AM TRAINED IN SILENT KILLING. MY GENIUS LIES IN THE ABILITY TO HUNT BY SOUND ALONE!

BLAST IT... I'VE BEEN SO WORRIED ABOUT NARUTO AND SASUKE, I HADN'T CONSIDERED...
...HOW LONG IT'S BEEN SINCE I HAD TO FIGHT UNDER CONDITIONS THIS ADVERSE!

I'VE GOT TO CALM DOWN... STAY SMART...
WHO WILL HE TARGET NEXT?!

READ THIS WAY

SHB

BAM
!
!!
TOO LATE!!
AIEEEEE!!

THAT'S SAKURA'S VOICE!! WHAT'S HAPPENED?!
WHAT THE HELL DOES KAKASHI THINK HE'S DOING?!!

HUFF
!!

KRUNCH
MY EYES ARE BEGINNING TO ADJUST TO THE ENVIRONMENT...

HUFF
I'VE GOT TO DO SOMETHING!
IF THIS KEEPS UP, WE'LL ALL BE IN SERIOUS TROUBLE!
PUFF

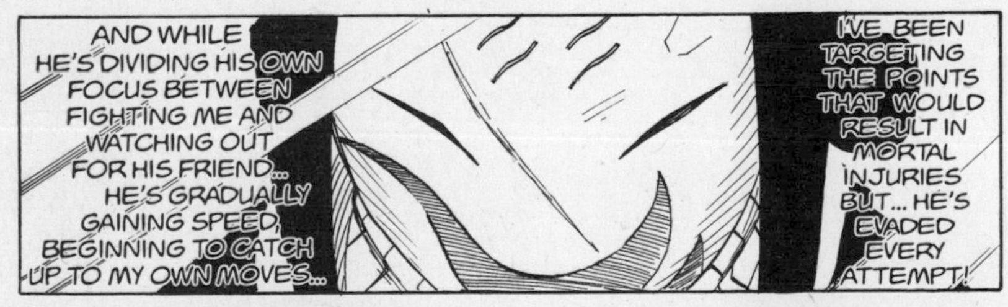
I'VE BEEN TARGETING THE POINTS THAT WOULD RESULT IN MORTAL INJURIES BUT... HE'S EVADED EVERY ATTEMPT!
AND WHILE HE'S DIVIDING HIS OWN FOCUS BETWEEN FIGHTING ME AND WATCHING OUT FOR HIS FRIEND... HE'S GRADUALLY GAINING SPEED, BEGINNING TO CATCH UP TO MY OWN MOVES...

THAT KID...
HE CAN SEE SOME-THING...!!

REAL NARUTO

Number 27: Awakenings

UHNGH...
SKFF

HE'S NARROWLY AVOIDING EVERY STRIKE I MAKE AT ONE OF HIS VULNERABLE SPOTS....
HIS MOVES ARE BRILLIANT!

YOU...
...MOVE WELL...

BUT MY NEXT ASSAULT WILL TAKE YOU DOWN!

SHF
HE SHOWS AMAZING STAMINA, REFLEXES, TRAINING, SKILL, AND JUDGEMENT......

FWSP
THOUGH HIS EVERY FACULTY MUST BE EXTENDED PAST ITS LIMIT BY NOW....

HERE HE COMES!!

STAY FROSTY... FOCUS...

CONCENTRATE...

AND LOOK THROUGH THE ILLUSION!!

HE WASN'T FOOLED... OR EVEN CONFUSED!
IMPOSSIBLE...!!

!

!!

HIS EYES ARE... IT CAN'T BE --!
THEY'RE... SHARINGAN...?!!

...YOU'RE...!!
I SEE... YOU, TOO, SHARE THE LEGACY OF A KEKKEI GENKAI BLOODLINE!

AN AMAZING BOY... A PRODIGY... STILL IN THE FLEDGLING STAGES...
IT WAS ONLY FOR A MOMENT... BUT I WAS ACTUALLY ABLE TO SEE!!!
TO FIND THAT ABILITY WITHIN HIMSELF AND FORCE IT TO AWAKEN, UNTUTORED, IN THE HEAT OF BATTLE--!

I CAN'T LET THIS FIGHT GO ON!
MY OWN ART FORCES ME TO EXPEND A GREAT DEAL OF CHAKRA, SO THERE IS A LIMIT TO HOW LONG I CAN GO ON USING IT!

AND I'M CERTAIN THAT THE LONGER OUR DUEL DRAGS ON...
THE GREATER YOUR ABILITY TO PERCEIVE MY MOVEMENTS WILL BECOME!
!
ESPECIALLY SINCE, TO A CERTAIN EXTENT, YOU CAN ALREADY SEE ME NOW!!
IT WOULD BE FOOLHARDY TO TRY TO TARGET YOU DIRECTLY...
...BUT IF I USE THE OTHER BOY AS BAIT.....
TIME TO BRING THIS TO AN END!!
!!
WHAT?! HE'S GOING AFTER NARUTO?!
NO! I HAVE TO GET THERE FIRST!!

DRIP DRIP

MASTER KAKASHI!!

!!

UHNN...

YOU WERE SLOW ON YOUR GUARD, KAKASHI!!
YOUR DESIRE TO SAVE THOSE BRATS CAUSED THE BLOOD TO RISE TO YOUR HEAD, OBSCURING YOUR THOUGHTS AND VISION AS SURELY AS THE FOG I'VE CREATED DOES!

...EVEN WITH YOUR IMPRESSIVE EYE AND THE FORMIDABLE POWERS YOU WIELD WITH IT...
YOUR ABILITY TO READ MY MOVEMENTS HAS BEEN BLUNTED!

HEH HEH HEH... I WANT TO ENJOY THIS, KAKASHI!
PAYING BACK WHAT YOU DID TO ME WOULD GIVE ME THE GREATEST PLEASURE!!

DON'T WORRY, HAKU SHOULD BE FINISHING OFF THOSE BRATS OF YOURS RIGHT ABOUT NOW...
KLAT

I'LL BE REUNITING YOU WITH THEM SHORTLY.
WHEN YOU MEET THEM IN THE AFTER-LIFE, BEG THEM TO FORGIVE YOU FOR YOUR WEAKNESS AND FOLLY!

HEH HEH HEH... HA HA HA HA HAA!!
...
...

SASUKE WON'T BE EASY FOR SOMEONE LIKE THAT MASKED KID TO DEFEAT!

YEAH!

YEAH!

YEAH!

INNER SAKURA

YEAH!

YEAH!

YEAH!

NEITHER WILL NARUTO!!

YOU'RE RIGHT...

...

!

I HAVE FAITH IN THEM AND IN THEIR STRENGTHS - NARUTO'S UNPREDICTABILITY...
AND SASUKE IS ONE OF THE MOST WORTHY HEIRS TO THE MOST SUPERIOR BLOODLINE OF KONOHAGAKURE VILLAGE!

READ THIS WAY

...!
YOU DON'T MEAN--

THAT'S RIGHT...
HIS FULL NAME IS UCHIHA SASUKE.

HE'S A NINJA GENIUS...
WHO CARRIES IN HIS GENES THE KEKKEI GENKAI OF CLAN UCHIHA!!

HE'S THE SOLE SURVIVING MEMBER OF THAT TRAGIC CLAN, EH...
NO WONDER HIS DEVELOP-MENT IS SO REMARK-ABLE...

FWUP

SO HE MAY INDEED BE HAKU'S EQUAL...
NO ONE HAS EVER PENETRATED THE SECRET OF HAKU'S TECHNIQUES... UNTIL NOW...
NO ONE...
SHHHH

HE'S GONE AGAIN!!
SAKURA, DON'T MOVE AN INCH.
I'LL FINISH THIS AS QUICKLY AS I CAN!

BUT... OH... OK!
TAK

DID YOU HEAR THAT, ZABUZA?
DO YOU TRULY BELIEVE, AFTER ALL OF THE HARDSHIPS, I'VE SURVIVED IN THIS WORLD ARMED ONLY WITH THE SHARINGAN?
TAK
SNAP

I TOO WAS ONCE A MEMBER OF A NINJA ASSASSIN CORPS.
SNAP
TUMP
I'LL SHOW YOU WHAT KIND OF SHINOBI I ONCE WAS...
THIS ISN'T SOMETHING I LEARNED WITH THE SHARINGAN. LET ME SHOW YOU MY OWN TRUE ART!

READ THIS WAY

SHEESH... NO MATTER HOW MANY TIMES I WARN YOU, NARUTO, YOU STILL KEEP GETTING IN MY WAY...

SASUKE! YOU...
!

NOW GET THAT LAME EXPRESSION OFF YOUR STUPID FACE...

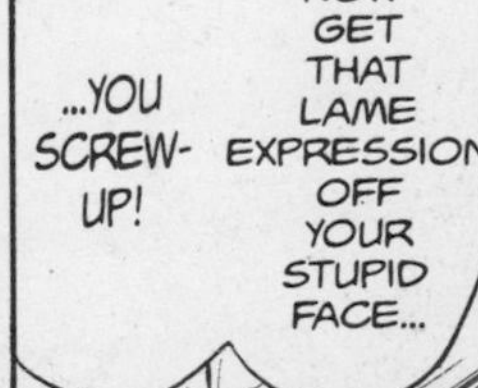
...YOU SCREW-UP!

...
WH- WHY...
HE WAS TRYING TO COVER ME...?!

GLARE—!!

HERE

YOU ASK ME WHY?

WHY...?!!

ARE YOU OKAY...

...YOU BIG CHICKEN?

TRY TO KEEP THAT IN MIND... DUNCE.

...BE A BETTER

THAT, AND LONELY.

WHAT?

BEING SCOLDED BY YOUR FOLKS DOESN'T EVEN COMPARE!

TOLD YOU IF YOU DIDN'T TAKE A BREAK YOU'D WEAR YOURSELF OUT, YOU DOPE.

READ THIS WAY

WHY... WHY DID YOU...?!
WHY...
ME...?

DRIP

YOU SHOULD HAVE JUST MINDED YOUR OWN BUSINESS!!

...HOW SHOULD I KNOW...?
GAK

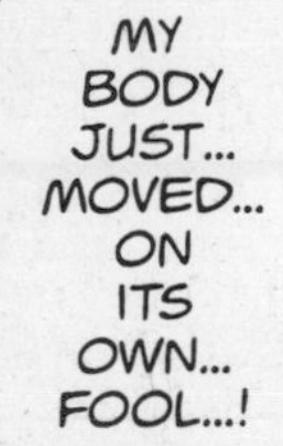
MY BODY JUST... MOVED... ON ITS OWN... FOOL...!

!

SFF

WHUD
!

READ THIS WAY

I SWORE I WOULDN'T DIE...
...UNTIL I KILLED HIM... MY OLDER BROTHER... THOUGHT THE OATH WOULD SAVE ME...BUT...

...BUT DON'T YOU DARE DIE...

!

RIPP

HE STRUCK ONE BLOW AT ME... AND WITHOUT ANY SIGN OF SHIRKING...
... SACRIFICED HIMSELF FOR YOU!!
SHFF
HE WAS A SHINOBI WORTHY OF THE UTMOST RESPECT...
...WHO IN ORDER TO PROTECT SOMEONE HE CARED ABOUT, THREW HIMSELF HEADLONG INTO WHAT HE KNEW FULL WELL WAS A TRAP.

READ THIS WAY

IS THIS THE FIRST TIME A COMRADE OF YOURS HAS DIED...?
SUCH IS A NINJA'S PATH.
SHFF

I USED TO HATE YOU, YOU KNOW...

I'M NEVER GONNA FORGIVE YOU FOR THIS...

I'M GONNA KILL YOU!!!

!!

TO BE CONTINUED IN ***NARUTO*** VOL.4!

IN THE NEXT VOLUME...

There comes a time in every ninja's training when he must put aside his morals and face the truth: *ninjas are tools for killing*. For Naruto, seeing Sasuke dead, that time is now. Rage awakens the nine-tailed fox spirit within Naruto, turning the tables on Haku...but can Naruto, Kakashi and Sakura take down the assassins without Sasuke's aid? And can the fox spirit, once unleashed, be put away?

AVAILABLE NOW!

Check us out on the web!

www.shonenjump.com

COMPLETE OUR SURVEY AND LET US KNOW WHAT YOU THINK!

☐ Please do NOT send me information about VIZ Media and SHONEN JUMP products, news and events, special offers, or other information.

☐ Please do NOT send me information from VIZ Media's trusted business partners.

Name: ______________________________

Address: ______________________________

City: ______________ **State:** ______ **Zip:** ______________

E-mail: ______________________________

☐ **Male** ☐ **Female** **Date of Birth (mm/dd/yyyy):** ___/___/_____ (**Under 13? Parental consent required.**)

1 Do you purchase SHONEN JUMP Magazine?

☐ Yes ☐ No

If **YES**, do you subscribe?

☐ Yes ☐ No

If **NO**, how often do you purchase SHONEN JUMP Magazine?

☐ 1-3 issues a year ☐ 4-6 issues a year ☐ more than 7 issues a year

2 Which SHONEN JUMP Manga did you purchase this time? (please check only one)

☐ Beet the Vandel Buster	☐ Bleach	☐ Bobobo-bo Bo-bobo
☐ Death Note	☐ Dragon Ball	☐ Dragon Ball Z
☐ Dr. Slump	☐ Eyeshield 21	☐ Hikaru no Go
☐ Hunter x Hunter	☐ I"s	☐ JoJo's Bizarre Adventure
☐ Knights of the Zodiac	☐ Legendz	☐ Naruto
☐ One Piece	☐ Rurouni Kenshin	☐ Shaman King
☐ The Prince of Tennis	☐ Ultimate Muscle	☐ Whistle!
☐ Yu-Gi-Oh!	☐ Yu-Gi-Oh!: Duelist	☐ Yu-Gi-Oh!: Millennium World
☐ YuYu Hakusho	☐ Other ______________	

Will you purchase subsequent volumes?

☐ Yes ☐ No

3 How did you learn about this title? (check all that apply)

☐ Favorite title	☐ Advertisement	☐ Article
☐ Gift	☐ Read excerpt in SHONEN JUMP Magazine	
☐ Recommendation	☐ Special offer	☐ Through TV animation
☐ Website	☐ Other ______________	

4 Of the titles that are serialized in SHONEN JUMP Magazine, have you purchased the paperback manga volumes?

☐ Yes ☐ No

If **YES**, which ones have you purchased? (check all that apply)

☐ Hikaru no Go ☐ Naruto ☐ One Piece ☐ Shaman King
☐ Yu-Gi-Oh!: Millennium World ☐ YuYu Hakusho

If **YES**, what were your reasons for purchasing? (please pick up to 3)

☐ A favorite title ☐ A favorite creator/artist ☐ I want to read it in one go
☐ I want to read it over and over again ☐ There are extras that aren't in the magazine
☐ The quality of printing is better than the magazine ☐ Recommendation
☐ Special offer ☐ Other

If **NO**, why did/would you not purchase it?

☐ I'm happy just reading it in the magazine ☐ It's not worth buying the manga volume
☐ All the manga pages are in black and white, unlike the magazine
☐ There are other manga volumes that I prefer ☐ There are too many to collect for each title
☐ It's too small ☐ Other ____________________

5 Of the titles NOT serialized in the magazine, which ones have you purchased?
(check all that apply)

☐ Beet the Vandel Buster ☐ Bleach ☐ Bobobo-bo Bo-bobo ☐ Death Note
☐ Dragon Ball ☐ Dragon Ball Z ☐ Dr. Slump ☐ Eyeshield 21
☐ Hunter x Hunter ☐ I"s ☐ JoJo's Bizarre Adventure ☐ Knights of the Zodiac
☐ Legendz ☐ The Prince of Tennis ☐ Rurouni Kenshin ☐ Ultimate Muscle
☐ Whistle! ☐ Yu-Gi-Oh! ☐ Yu-Gi-Oh!: Duelist ☐ None
☐ Other ____________________

If you did purchase any of the above, what were your reasons for purchasing?

☐ A favorite title ☐ A favorite creator/artist
☐ Read a preview in SHONEN JUMP Magazine and wanted to read the rest of the story
☐ Recommendation ☐ Other

Will you purchase subsequent volumes?

☐ Yes ☐ No

6 What race/ethnicity do you consider yourself? (please check one)

☐ Asian/Pacific Islander ☐ Black/African American ☐ Hispanic/Latino
☐ Native American/Alaskan Native ☐ White/Caucasian ☐ Other

THANK YOU! Please send the completed form to:

VIZ Media Survey
42 Catharine St.
Poughkeepsie, NY 12601

VIZ media

All information provided will be used for internal purposes only. We promise not to sell or otherwise divulge your information.